Calvin Coolidge

30th President of the United States

This picture of President Coolidge was taken on the south lawn of the White House just before he was inaugurated on March 4, 1925. He had already served as President for a year and seven months. (Library of Congress.)

Calvin Coolidge
30th President of the United States

Rita Stevens

 GARRETT EDUCATIONAL CORPORATION

Cover: *Official presidential portrait of Calvin Coolidge by Charles S. Hopkinson.* (Copyrighted by the White House Historical Association; photograph by the National Geographic Society.)

Manufactured in the United States of America

Edited and produced by Synthegraphics Corporation

Library of Congress Cataloging in Publication Data

Stevens, Rita.
  Calvin Coolidge, 30th president of the United States / Rita Stevens.
      p.   cm. — (Presidents of the United States)
  Includes bibliographical references.
  Summary: Presents the life of Calvin Coolidge, including his childhood, education, employment, and political career.
  1. Coolidge, Calvin, 1872–1933 — Juvenile literature.
2. Presidents — United States — Biography — Juvenile literature.   3. United States — Politics and government — 1923–1929 — Juvenile literature.   [1. Coolidge, Calvin, 1872–1933.   2. Presidents.]
I. Title   II. Title: Calvin Coolidge, thirtieth president of the United States.   III. Series.
E792.S74   1990
973.91'5'092 — dc20   CHILDRENS ROOM
[B]
[92]   89-39949
ISBN 0-944483-57-7   CIP
                                                       AC

Contents

Chronology for Calvin Coolidge

1872 Born on July 4 in Plymouth, Vermont

1891– 1895 Attended Amherst College in Amherst, Massachusetts

1897 Opened law practice in Northampton, Massachusetts

1899 Elected to city council of Northampton

1900– 1901 Served as city solicitor of Northampton

1903– 1904 Served as clerk of courts for Hampshire County

1905 Married Grace Anna Goodhue on October 4

1907– 1908 Served two terms in Massachusetts state legislature

1910– 1911 Served as mayor of Northampton

1912– 1915 Held a seat in Massachusetts state senate; senate president 1914–1915

1916– 1918 Served as lieutenant governor of Massachusetts

1919– 1920 Served as governor of Massachusetts

1921 Became Vice-President under Warren G. Harding

1923 Became President on August 3 upon Harding's death

1924 Was elected President

1929 Retired from political life

1933 Died in Northampton on January 5

Chapter 1

The Battle in Boston

A s the afternoon of Tuesday, September 9, 1919, lengthened into dusk, the busy city streets of Boston emptied as if by magic. Normally, the state capital of Massachusetts was lively at all hours. As the biggest city in New England, it had stores with attractive windows, cafes, and park benches to tempt the crowds of workers streaming homeward or the families strolling along together. But on this particular afternoon, mothers nervously herded their children indoors; workers hurried home with quick glances from side to side; tenants fearfully bolted their doors.

POLICE ON STRIKE

The city was covered by a looming cloud of doubt and fear. No one knew what was going to happen that night, but everyone feared the worst. Earlier that day, Boston's 1,136 policemen had gone out on strike. They had refused to return to work until the city allowed them to organize a labor union, the purpose of which would be to insist on higher wages and better working conditions in Boston's police department.

Many Bostonians agreed that the police deserved higher pay and better working conditions; some of these citizens even agreed that the police had the right to form a union. But as conflict between the policemen and the city government developed during early September, most of these people did not believe that their friendly neighborhood policemen would make good on their threat to strike.

Now, as darkness gathered over Boston, the citizens knew otherwise. That comforting policeman with his nightstick tucked under his arm no longer patrolled the street outside. The great city lay helpless, with no one to enforce the law or protect the weak except a hundred or so untrained and unarmed volunteer guards. Many of the guards were students from Harvard College in nearby Cambridge.

The Night of the Mob

Night fell. The streets remained quiet for a time. It was as though the ghost of the policeman's authority lingered on to maintain order. Then, slowly at first, the ghost of authority faded and the city came to restless life.

It started with small bands of boys and men, roaming the streets just to see what was going on. They talked and laughed among themselves, more and more loudly. These bands joined to form larger groups, and the talk and laughter became shouts and high-pitched yelps. No policeman appeared to quiet them. Before long, knots of people gathered to shoot dice, which was illegal in Boston, in the pool of yellow radiance shed by every streetlight. No policeman appeared to break up the game.

Beer and whiskey bottles were passed from hand to hand. Public drinking was also illegal, but no policeman appeared to hustle the drinkers off to jail. Then, sometime around midnight, the roving, gambling, drinking gangs in all parts of the city came together to form a single, huge, uncontrollable mob.

The mob suddenly realized its own strength at one o'clock in the morning, when someone threw a stone through a shop window. The crash of breaking glass gave the rioters a new idea: looting. Stores and offices were unprotected. The goods of Boston were there for the taking—after all, with no policemen, what could happen to a looter or burglar? The volunteer guards were not only few in number, they were also terrified and helpless. A hailstorm of sticks and stones shattered windows all over the city, and the free-for-all was on.

Fights broke out among the rioters. Fortunately, no one was killed or badly injured, either in the mob or in the buildings that were looted. No one is sure just how much property was damaged or stolen in the course of that eventful night, but when dawn rose over the city, at least $60,000 worth of broken or discarded loot lay strewn across the streets. The shaken Bostonians emerged timidly from their homes to see a city that looked as if it had been invaded by a hostile army.

Opposing Leaders

During the weeks that led up to the strike, two men had been engaged in a battle of their own. They were Boston's mayor, Andrew J. Peters, and the governor of Massachusetts, Calvin Coolidge. Each man had his own ideas about how the threat of a police strike should be handled, and they were in opposition from the first.

Mayor Peters was fearful of any trouble in the city that might cost him popularity among the voters and lose him future elections. He did not want to make enemies of the police, but he also wanted the worried citizens of Boston to know that he stood for law and order. So his general approach was to try to please all parties in the dispute and to take as little personal responsibility for events as he possibly could. He tried repeatedly to push the responsibility for handling the police situation over to the governor's office.

Governor Coolidge, on the other hand, felt that the safe operation of the city was first of all the mayor's responsibility (that was, in fact, the case). Coolidge was determined not to take any action in the matter until the mayor had exercised his rightful authority. Unlike Peters, however, Coolidge had a strong, even unshakable belief about the rights and wrongs of the situation.

The governor was genuinely sympathetic to the plight of the underpaid policemen. In fact, he said to a group of newspaper reporters, "Can you blame the police for feeling as they do when they get less than a street-car conductor?" But above and beyond that sympathy, he believed that *no one* had the right to strike if such a strike would endanger public safety and the law. To Coolidge, a policeman who walked off his job was not a worker striking for better pay—he was a soldier who deserted his post in battle.

Disobedience in the Police Force

The unrest in the Boston police department came to a head just days before the strike, when 19 police officers went on trial for disobeying the city's police commissioner. The commissioner had ordered the officers not to join the American Federation of Labor (AFL), which was the nation's largest group of labor unions. But the 19 officers defied the order and joined the AFL. Then they were tried for disobedience to the commissioner and found guilty. When they were dismissed from the department, the entire police force threatened to strike.

The mayor begged Governor Coolidge to overrule the commissioner and restore the officers to the police force if

Governor Coolidge (left) and the Boston police commissioner were united in their opposition to the strike by the city's policemen. Together they took control of the situation from Mayor Peters. (Library of Congress.)

they would agree to resign from the AFL. But Coolidge, who was nothing if not stubborn, stood by the police commissioner. As much as he sympathized with the policemen, he cared more about law and order. He feared that if he gave in to the threat of a strike on this occasion, Boston would, in the future, be held hostage to the demands of any group of striking workers.

This had happened in other American cities in 1919, and Coolidge did not want it happening in his state. So he kept quiet—something he was good at all through his life—and let events take their course. Coolidge had no intention of saving Mayor Peters from the need to take action, but he was prepared to take firm action of his own when the time was right.

The Second Night

All during Wednesday, the day after the nighttime riot, Boston wondered what would happen that night. The city's firemen were now threatening to go out on strike along with their friends in the police department. To many people, such talk was simply an invitation to the mobs to burn the city down.

Mayor Peters fretted, wishing that someone would take things out of his hands. Coolidge waited calmly. Finally, Peters did the only thing he could do. Using the authority granted to him under an old municipal law, he ordered all members of the State Guard who were stationed in the city to go on active duty that night.

There were not enough uniformed guardsmen to replace the entire police force. But the guardsmen were armed and trained as a military unit, so they were quite effective against an undisciplined, unarmed mob. When the crowds of looters surged into the streets after dark, they encountered an unpleasant surprise.

Thursday morning's *Boston Herald* read:

RIOTS AND BLOODSHED
IN CITY AS STATE
GUARD QUELLS MOB

Riotous mobs bent on plundering and destruction of property attempted last night to plunge Boston into a turmoil of crime and general disorder; and only sobered down and went home after the State Guard had fired into a crowd at South Boston, killing two men and wounding nine, and cavalry had charged into a crowd at Scollay Square with drawn sabers, scattering it in all directions.

The Governor Takes Charge

At last Mayor Peters had taken action. The result, however, was a bloody and tragic disaster. But now Coolidge feared that Peters, having had a taste of authority, might go so far as to give their jobs back to the 19 police officers who had been fired. This would undo everything that the governor and the police commissioner had tried to accomplish in sticking to the strict letter of the law. Furthermore, Coolidge did not want Peters, whom he disliked and with whom he disagreed on many issues, to become a popular hero. If there was any heroism to be had from this sad business, Coolidge thought, *he* was more deserving of it.

So, now that the city government had done its part, Coolidge finally decided to exert the state's authority. He issued two orders. One called out the State Guard from all over the state for duty in Boston, and the other took direct control of the police force in Boston, putting Peters out of the picture. After two distressing nights of violence, the police strike was firmly in the hands of the governor.

A NATIONAL HERO

That Thursday afternoon Governor Coolidge seized control of the Boston government and appointed the police commissioner as his lieutenant. This action made Coolidge a national hero. At a time when most middle-class Americans feared the disruptions and violence of labor strikes as much as they feared the plague, Coolidge looked like the man of the hour, meeting both strikers and mobs with iron resistance. Newspapers in almost every city in the country ran his picture. Suddenly, Calvin Coolidge was no longer just the little-known, quiet governor of an eastern state. People across the

Samuel Gompers founded the American Federation of Labor, the nation's biggest labor union. Coolidge became nationally famous when he said to Gompers, "There is no right to strike against the public safety by anybody, anywhere, any time." (Library of Congress.)

land came to recognize his lean, keen-eyed face; his down-turned mouth; and his high, broad forehead.

And soon Coolidge provided a heroic slogan to go with his national image. He announced that the policemen who had gone on strike would *not* be allowed to have their jobs back under any circumstances. When Samuel Gompers, head of the AFL, pleaded with Governor Coolidge to reconsider this decision, claiming that workers must be allowed the right to strike, Coolidge replied, "There is no right to strike against the public safety by anybody, anywhere, any time." These words were echoed in all the nation's newspapers.

The majority of Americans were comforted by Coolidge's confident statement, which restored their belief in law and order. Many of these people began to feel that a man who had withstood such a crisis in Boston might be a good addition to the national government in Washington. Although he claimed he had never dreamed of a higher honor than being governor of Massachusetts, Calvin Coolidge — the hero of the Boston police strike — would soon be on his way to the White House.

Chapter 2

Vermont Values

Calvin Coolidge was born and brought up in a small town in Vermont. Throughout his life, people called him a "typical New Englander" because he demonstrated traits that were believed to be characteristic of people from New England, especially Vermont. For example, Vermonters were generally thought of as quiet people who spoke little, and Coolidge was a man of few words—in fact, his quietness was the basis of many jokes during and after his presidency. When they *did* speak, though, Vermonters were credited with wit and humor, and Coolidge's few words were often very funny indeed. Furthermore, New Englanders were sometimes thought to be very thrifty, even tightfisted with money, and Coolidge's economical ways became legendary.

NEW ENGLAND ROOTS

Beneath these outward traits, Coolidge had deeper qualities. He valued independent thinking, self-reliance, and hard work. He believed that a man should save for the future and keep his word. He disapproved of boasting, luxury, and wastefulness. Many historians and authors who have written about Coolidge have said that these values were typical of 19th-century New England.

For the most part, New England was a region of independent farms and small rural communities, not of cities and factories. Many families produced all of their own food, clothes, tools, and furniture, so people learned to depend upon themselves, to work diligently, and to make things last a long time. In addition, New England preserved the heritage of the Puritans, the English Protestants who had come to the American colonies in the 17th century seeking the freedom to follow their own religious beliefs. The Puritan way of life and thought stressed simplicity, orderliness, and duty to God and one's fellow man. These values lingered on in New England. They were part of Coolidge's Vermont heritage.

In 1855, a generation before Coolidge was born, a New England newspaper editor named Horace Greeley had advised young men who were eager to make a name for themselves to turn to the West, that great region that was just then being opened up to settlement, commerce, and politics. "Go west, young man, go west," Greeley is often believed to have said. In fact, those were *not* his exact words, but because they captured his thoughts and the spirit of the times, they were frequently repeated. However, Calvin Coolidge's steadfast New England spirit was captured in a remark he made as President to a reporter: "The Coolidges never went West." The sweeping plains and towering peaks of the West held no appeal for Coolidge. All his life, he remained deeply attached to his New England roots.

FAMILY BACKGROUND

Coolidge's ancestors were English, Scottish, and Welsh. But the Coolidge family had been part of American history since the earliest days of the colonies. Calvin's distant ancestor, John

Coolidge of Cambridgeshire, England, came to the colonies sometime around 1630. He settled in Watertown, Massachusetts. His descendants were still living in Massachusetts 150 years later, when the colonies declared their independence from Great Britain. Calvin's great-great-grandfather, John Coolidge, fought at the Battle of Lexington during the Revolutionary War. It is not known for certain just when this revolutionary soldier came north, but he did move to Vermont. He settled near the small town of Plymouth and established the Coolidge clan there.

The Coolidges of Plymouth bought land, built homes and barns, and farmed. Some of them were storekeepers. They were never spectacularly wealthy, but by the standards of small-town Vermont, they were comfortably well off. They were also community leaders. At one time or another, nearly all of Calvin Coolidge's Vermont ancestors served as justices of the peace, aldermen (town councilmen), town clerks, members of the state legislature, and deacons of the Congregational Church. This interest in public affairs — and the sense that it was his responsibility to participate in them — was also part of Calvin's heritage.

A 4th of July Baby

Calvin's father was John Calvin Coolidge, a farmer and storekeeper in the community called Plymouth Notch, an outlying part of Plymouth. He had fought in the Army of the North during the Civil War, earning the rank of colonel; throughout his later life, friends called him Colonel Coolidge.

In 1868, when he was 23 years old, the colonel married Victoria Josephine Moor. The Moor family had moved from the Connecticut River Valley to a town called Pinney Hollow in Vermont. President Coolidge later said that, accord-

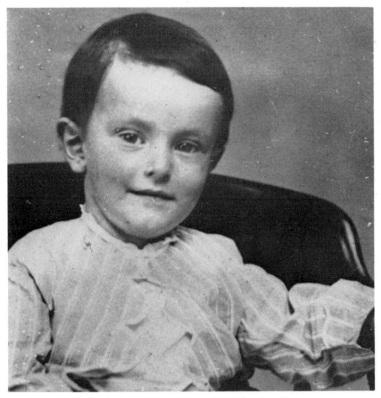

Young Calvin is shown here at age three, about the time his sister Abbie was born. (Forbes Library.)

ing to Moor family stories, his mother had some American Indian ancestry, but no records to prove this claim have survived.

In 1872, four years after Colonel Coolidge married Victoria Moor, she gave birth to a son. The boy was born on July 4, so that his birthday was always celebrated along with the nation's most patriotic holiday. He was named John Calvin Coolidge after his father. To avoid confusion in the household, though, he was almost always called "Calvin" or "Cal."

Years later, when he graduated from college, the young man officially dropped the "John" from his name. As an adult, he preferred to be called "Calvin." He was sometimes called "Cal"—but seldom to his face, because he made it clear that he did not like the shortened version of his name.

Calvin was born in the family home, a five-room cottage that was attached to his father's general store. Three years later, a second child was born there. Calvin's sister was named Abigail Gratia, but she was always called "Abbie."

An Early Loss

Young Calvin adored his mother, whom he remembered as fair-haired and delicate. She loved poetry and flowers, and she planted a flowerbed in the yard, next to a clump of fragrant lilac bushes. Calvin said of her later that "there was a touch of mysticism and poetry in her nature which made her love to gaze at the purple sunsets and watch the evening stars."

Sadly, this sensitive, gentle woman became ill around the time of Abbie's birth. She appears to have suffered from tuberculosis, a disease of the lungs that causes its victims to become increasingly weak. She died when Calvin was 12 years old. He remembered that she called him and Abbie to her bedside, where the children received a final blessing from their mother. "In an hour she was gone," he recalled. "We laid her away in the blustering snows of March. The greatest grief that can come to a boy came to me. Life was never the same again."

Calvin's sorrow over his mother's death was deep and long-lasting. He carried a small picture of her inside his pocket watch until the day of his death, and he confessed to friends that he often daydreamed about her.

Plymouth Boyhood

In spite of the sickness and death of his mother, Calvin en-joyed a normal childhood, one that was not especially gloomy or haunted by grief. One important and colorful figure in his early childhood was his grandfather, old Calvin Galusha Coolidge, who was called "Galoosh." Grandfather Coolidge's house was surrounded by a garden full of bright poppies, and he always had plenty of horses and puppies around. He even had a peacock, which delighted young Calvin with its bril-liant blue-and-green plumy tail. Grandfather Coolidge taught Calvin how to ride a horse, even to ride standing up like a circus performer. When he was old enough, Calvin had a horse of his own, a calico that he loved.

Grandfather Coolidge also helped Calvin's mother teach the boy how to read at a very young age, using the Bible for a textbook. And when Calvin's father, Colonel Coolidge, was elected to the state legislature in Montpelier, Vermont, Grand-father Coolidge took the three-year-old Calvin and his mother to Montpelier to see the statehouse. Legend says that the old man even sat the child in the governor's chair for a treat, but Calvin remembered little of that and only recalled being im-pressed by the stuffed animals with which the statehouse was decorated. He especially remembered one mountain lion, which, he said, looked ready to jump at him.

For his part, Calvin Galusha Coolidge was very fond of his grandson. He died when Calvin was six. His will re-vealed that he had left a 40-acre farm and some livestock to Calvin. Grandfather Coolidge must have expected his grand-son to carry on the family tradition of farming in Plymouth, and he wanted to make certain that the boy had a farm to call his own. But Calvin's future lay outside Plymouth, and he never did work that farm.

Plymouth, Vermont, looked like this – serene and rural – during Coolidge's boyhood. He enjoyed typical country pastimes such as horseback riding and fishing. (Library of Congress.)

Doing Family Chores

Calvin's childhood was much like that of any other boy in rural 19th-century America. Almost as soon as he could walk, he had chores to do on his father's farm, such as gathering eggs laid by the hens and picking fruit. As he became older and stronger, he graduated to harder tasks, such as plowing the fields with an ox-drawn plow, planting crops, and stacking firewood.

Like other Vermont families, the Coolidges had a "sugar camp" in the forest where they spent several weeks every spring drawing sap from the sugar maple trees to make maple syrup. Calvin took this job seriously and was said to be better than any boy around at getting sap out of the trees. He was also clever with his hands. He learned to use a pocketknife before he could read, and he carved bows and arrows from hickory and ash wood. He was also good at making kites.

In those days, recreation was as vigorous as work. Calvin skated on frozen ponds in the winter and swam in them in the summer. He hunted and trapped in the wooded hills, often hiking many miles in a day, and he fished in the streams (in later life, fishing was one of his few relaxations). All of this activity made young Calvin strong and fit, although he was never tall or muscular. He had red hair, freckles, and blue eyes.

"Silent Cal"

Although he was fairly ordinary as a child, Calvin did have one noteworthy quality. He was unusually quiet and seldom spoke up unless he had something important to say—and then he used as few words as possible. This trait remained with him all his life, earning him the nickname "Silent Cal."

One reason for Calvin's quietness was that he was shy and uncomfortable around strangers and people he did not know well. Many years later, speaking of his childhood, Coolidge said:

> When I was a little fellow, as long ago as I can remember, I would go into a panic if I heard strange voices in the kitchen. I felt I just couldn't meet the people and shake hands with them. . . . The hardest thing in the world was to go through the door and give them a greeting. I was almost ten before I realized I couldn't go on that way. And by fighting hard I used to manage to get through that door. I'm all right with old friends, but every time I meet a stranger, I've got to go through the old kitchen door, back home, and it's not easy.

Frugality and Religion

During his childhood, Calvin learned the value of money. Although Colonel Coolidge earned a comfortable living, he believed in saving money, not in spending it. The Coolidges never wasted anything, and they accounted for every penny they spent. Young Calvin earned a little money by selling apples and popcorn balls at town meetings. His father encouraged him to save it, and he did. The habit of saving remained with him throughout his life, and so did the practice of knowing where and how every cent was spent. To some, these ways would seem miserly and cheap; to others, they appeared sensible and economical.

Religion also played a part in Calvin's childhood. Like most of their neighbors, the Coolidges were members of a Congregational Church, one of many such small Protestant churches that lifted trim white spires above the rolling green hills of Vermont. The Coolidges were not especially religious, but they did believe that regular Sunday church attendance and participation in church affairs were necessary parts of good living and good citizenship.

EDUCATION OF A YOUNG REPUBLICAN

Calvin's education started at home with the reading lessons given by his mother and grandfather. When he was five, he started attending the local elementary school and stayed there until he was 13. He was just an ordinary student, with grades perhaps a bit above the average.

When Calvin was 13, he graduated from the town school by passing the same test that his teacher had to pass in order to get the schoolteaching job. As a student, he was almost never late or absent — a characteristic that stayed with him throughout his career.

During his childhood, Calvin had been taken on several trips to such nearby towns as Woodstock, Montpelier, and Rutland. But his first real experience of life outside Plymouth came in 1886, when he went away to school at the age of 14. His father had attended Black River Academy, a private high school for boys in Ludlow, Vermont, about 12 miles from Plymouth. Calvin went there in his turn.

Going to the academy for the first time was a big event in Calvin's life — his first real separation from home and family. Much later he wrote that the preparations and packing for his first trip to Ludlow were more time-consuming than those that occurred when he left the White House. Colonel Coolidge hitched a horse to the wagon and drove his son to Ludlow, then turned around and went home through the October snow. For three years, all the while Calvin was at Black River, the colonel made that same journey nearly every weekend during the school year to visit his son.

Black River Boy

Calvin's classes at Black River Academy were much like those of any young man in a good school at the time. He studied Latin, algebra (and a little geometry), American history, and

English grammar. He also studied rhetoric, the art of using language persuasively in speaking or writing. He sharpened this skill by writing essays, and he joined the school's debating groups. He did well at both, although he never became really noteworthy as a writer or a speech-maker.

Education did not end when Calvin left the classroom. During his years at Black River, he was an eager reader. When he went home to Plymouth for weekend or summer visits, he read all of his father's and grandfather's books. His favorites were two action-packed tales of Vermont adventure and patriotism, *The Rangers* and *The Green Mountain Boys* by D. M. Thompson. He also enjoyed a book called *Livingstone Lost and Found,* by the Reverend Josiah Tyler, which was an account of the travels of a Scottish missionary, David Livingstone, in Africa.

Calvin did not often take part in sports or games while he was at Black River. Instead, he worked. At home, he spent one summer painting the fences and outbuildings and doing repairs on the family farm. And in Ludlow he spent many Saturdays working in a local toy factory, where he was paid a small sum for each toy wagon he made. He added these earnings to his savings.

Another Family Loss

The deaths of his grandfather and of his mother had been sorrowful burdens for young Calvin. During his last year at Black River, he endured yet another loss. His younger sister, Abbie, died of a severe illness that probably was appendicitis, which doctors of the day did not know how to treat. Calvin spent a day and a night at her bedside before her death and grieved deeply when she died.

In the summer of 1890, Calvin was graduated from Black River Academy. His graduating class consisted of nine people. Calvin was the class secretary and gave one of the commencement speeches. He had hoped to go to Amherst College in Massachusetts, but he failed the entrance examinations, possibly because he was ill.

Whatever the reason for the failure, Calvin spent the winter of 1890–1891 at St. Johnsbury Academy in Ludlow. There he took a special course designed to prepare students to enter college. He passed this course in the spring of 1891— which meant that he was qualified to enter Amherst the following fall.

Political Excitement

The idea of going away to college was exciting, but that summer held some political excitement as well. Sometime around his 19th birthday, Calvin accompanied his father to Bennington, Vermont, to hear President Benjamin Harrison speak. The President, a Civil War hero and a Republican, was extremely popular in Vermont, where most voters belonged to the Republican Party. He had been invited to Bennington to dedicate a new monument and was accompanied by many of the notable Republican leaders of the day, including the governor of Vermont, two Cabinet members, and at least one Republican general from the Civil War.

Because Calvin's father and grandfather had been state legislators, the Coolidges were entitled to a place inside the large tent where a banquet was served in the President's honor. Throughout the grand occasion, Calvin remained humbly quiet and called no attention to himself. Yet he was busy observing and listening, and he was impressed by the calm, bearded President. Calvin later described the impression that the President made on him this way: "As I looked on him and realized that he personally represented the glory and dignity of the United States, I wondered how it felt to bear so much responsibility, and little thought that I would ever know."

Chapter 3

College Years

The year 1891 was a significant one for the Coolidge family. In addition to the excitement of seeing President Benjamin Harrison at Bennington, that year brought a new member into the family. It had been six years since the death of Calvin's mother, and now his father was ready to remarry. His bride was Carrie A. Brown, a Plymouth schoolteacher. Calvin grew quite fond of his stepmother. He was glad to see his father happy and to know that the colonel would not be alone when his son went off to college.

AMHERST COLLEGE

College was the next step in young Coolidge's life. In the fall of 1891 he moved south to the small town of Amherst, in central Massachusetts, to begin his studies at Amherst College. It was the first time he had left his home state of Vermont.

Amherst College was a good choice for a young man from a thrifty family—and with only slightly better than average grades. It was not in the first rank of East Coast schools, such as Harvard, Yale, and Princeton, but it was highly regarded for its fine library and for the good quality of its teachers and the education they gave.

The college had been founded in 1821 by a group of noteworthy New Englanders that included Noah Webster, creator of the first great American dictionary. The founders of the college had all been Congregationalists, members of the same New England Protestant church to which the Coolidge family belonged, and for many years Amherst was known as the college at which Congregationalist ministers received their educations. Until shortly before Coolidge's time, in fact, nearly half of the young men who graduated from the college entered the ministry. Although it does not seem that Coolidge ever considered becoming a minister, his years at Amherst did have a spiritual side that deeply influenced his later life and his career in politics.

An Inspiring Teacher

That spiritual element was due to one man in particular—Professor Charles E. Garman, who taught philosophy at Amherst. Garman was Coolidge's favorite teacher. He was tall and thin, and his coal-black eyes seemed to glow with enthusiasm whenever a classroom discussion grew especially interesting. He was a favorite of many of the Amherst students, and he remained on friendly terms with a number of them after they left school. Coolidge was one such student; another was Harlan F. Stone, who attended Amherst at the same time Coolidge did. Years later, Coolidge was to appoint Stone to a seat on the U.S. Supreme Court.

Coolidge, Stone, and the other students found Garman's classes stimulating and exciting. Garman did not simply lecture from behind a wooden pulpit as most teachers did. Instead, his lectures were mixed with informal talks in which everyone was invited to participate. He asked the students questions about their beliefs and values. He decorated the classroom walls with mottoes and slogans that were designed to start discussions between students who agreed with them and those who disagreed. But Garman was also a very religious man whose belief in God communicated itself to his students.

Garman's teaching was important to Coolidge in several ways. First, Garman encouraged him to think for himself and to have confidence in his own thoughts and beliefs. For the rest of his life, Coolidge was a man who liked to make up his own mind on every issue and whose opinions remained firm and unshakable. Second, Garman filled many of his students—including Coolidge—with the desire to devote themselves to public service. Garman taught his students that people who had the benefits of a higher education also had a duty to society. It was their responsibility to improve the lives of their fellow citizens, through teaching, preaching, social work, or some other service. This philosophy helped guide Calvin Coolidge into politics.

An Average Student

As inspiring as they were, Garman's classes in philosophy were only part of Coolidge's experience at Amherst. He studied calculus, an advanced course in mathematics that all students were required to take. His other classes included Greek, Italian, history, and English literature. The college offered some courses in the natural sciences, and Coolidge received his worst grade, a D, in his physics class. Throughout college, his grades remained average, mostly Bs and Cs. The grades improved a bit during his junior and senior years, when he took a special interest in rhetoric, philosophy, history, and debating. American history was one of his favorite courses, and fellow students recalled that he spent much of his free time in the library, eagerly poring over the writings of such early American leaders as John Adams and Alexander Hamilton. There were also exercise classes in the gymnasium, where the boys worked out with dumbbells and did sit-ups.

Sports were popular on the campus, but Coolidge had never been much of an athlete, and he did not participate in any of the college athletic activities. By now he had reached his full adult height: about five feet, nine inches. He was slender, though strong for his size. His features were pleasant but undistinguished. His most noticeable feature was his eyes; they were small and deep-set, but they were a lively blue. The bright red hair of his childhood had begun to fade into a less vivid medium brown shade, and his freckles were fading also.

In manner, Coolidge was quiet, serious, and rather slow to make friends. Forty years later, Harlan Stone described Coolidge as he was during his Amherst days:

> I doubt if many of his fellow students were intimate with him. His extreme reticence [reluctance to speak] made that difficult. To those who knew him casually he seemed odd or queer, but it only required a slight acquaintance to appreciate his quiet dignity and the self-respect which commanded the respect of others.

Social Life at Amherst

Amherst College was for young men only. But only an hour away by horse and buggy, or 15 minutes by train, was the town of Northampton, where a women's college called Smith was located. Amherst students often attended dances and parties at Smith, but Coolidge did not participate in such activities — at least not during his first few years of college.

On the Amherst campus itself, the young men's social life was dominated by fraternities, or private clubs. There were eight or nine fraternities at Amherst when Coolidge arrived at the college as a freshman. About three-fourths of all the students were invited to become members of one of the fraternities. Those students who readily received invitations were the sons of wealthy or prominent families, the good athletes, the distinguished students, and those with elegant social skills. These popular young men were quickly gathered into the fraternities. The others, those who did not find membership in a fraternity, were called "oudens," a slang term for "outsiders."

For three years, Coolidge was an "ouden." It seemed that he offered little to attract the fraternities. His family was an important part of the community back home in Plymouth, but that carried little weight at a school where the sons of many nationally prominent New England families were among the students. And he was neither an athlete, a distinguished student, nor a witty, popular conversationalist. Furthermore, he was on a tight budget. He had little to spend on clothes and entertainment, and he lived in a $3.50-a-week room in a boardinghouse that was located rather far from the heart of the campus.

Coolidge's reaction to being an "ouden" is typical of his stubborn determination and quiet self-confidence. It is clear that he wanted to join a fraternity. While he was still at Black River Academy, he had written to tell his father that he hoped he would be able to get into a fraternity when he started at Amherst. "Of course I want to join one if I can," he had said. Yet although he must have been disappointed and even hurt at not being chosen, there is no evidence to show that he felt anger or bitterness. Instead, he calmly turned his energies in other directions.

One of those directions was politics. In 1892, he joined the college's Republican Club. That year, Republican President Benjamin Harrison, whose appearance in Bennington the year before had made such a powerful impression on Coolidge, was running for re-election against the Democrat Grover Cleveland. With the other young Republicans, Coolidge attended meetings and speeches and took part in a torchlight parade around campus and through town. Although Harrison was defeated and the Democrats came into power that year, Coolidge's loyalty to the Republican Party was firmly established.

A Turning Point

The shyness that had troubled Coolidge as a little boy in his father's kitchen lingered on. His favorite pastime was taking long, solitary walks in the lovely wooded hills around Amherst, but he recognized that he must take advantage of the opportunity while at college to make social contacts and gain social skills. He had begun to plan a career in law—perhaps he had already begun to think of politics. So he battled his shyness and set out to attend every college function that was open to him. It was at such a function, during his junior year, that he began to make a name for himself with his fellow students.

It was an Amherst tradition for the junior class to put on a humorous foot race, in which the men had to run while wearing top hats, the tall black silk hats that were normally worn only for very formal occasions. Somehow Coolidge got hold of such a hat, and he entered the race, even though he was a poor runner. Not only did he not win, he came in last.

But Calvin turned losing into winning, because the loser traditionally had to give a speech. These speeches were generally not very memorable. Coolidge, however, had begun to do well in public speaking and debating, subjects that all students were required to study at the time. So at the conclusion of the race he surprised his classmates by delivering a funny speech, based on the line from the Bible that says that "the last shall be first and the first shall be last." His speech was greeted with enthusiastic applause from the crowd. That moment was the turning point in Coolidge's college experience—and perhaps in the whole course of his life. It proved to him that he had the ability to get people to listen to him and to win them over.

An "Ouden" No Longer

During his senior year, Coolidge was invited to join the Phi Gamma Delta fraternity, a new society that was seeking members at Amherst. His acceptance was typical for Coolidge—it was calm, collected, and brief. He listened in silence while two representatives of the fraternity made elaborate speeches of invitation and welcome. Then he simply said, "Yes."

Unlike many of his fellow "oudens," Coolidge had never attacked the fraternity system or turned against fraternity members in anger, because he believed that it made more sense in the long run to be on good terms with them. Now his patience had paid off. He was an "ouden" no longer. He also made one close friend during this time. Dwight Morrow, who was one of the outstanding students of Coolidge's class, had grown to admire and like Calvin, and the two men became lifelong friends. President Coolidge would later make Morrow his ambassador to Mexico.

The Campus Wit

Coolidge achieved a sort of mild popularity during his final year at Amherst. Not only was he asked to join Phi Gamma Delta, but after his speech on the day of the top hat race, he also gained a reputation as the campus wit, a funny speaker who could be counted on to provide laughs. Because of this reputation, he was asked to give a humorous speech, traditionally called the Grove Oration, on the day of his graduation from college.

Only three senior class members gave speeches that day, and Coolidge—the former nobody—was one of them. He did not graduate at the top of his 76-member class, or even near it, but he must have felt some pride in what he had achieved. He had completed a college education, he had joined a fraternity, and he had overcome his shyness to become the campus humorist. Now it was time to look toward the future.

Many years later, Dwight Morrow described that graduation day in the spring of 1895. When the speeches and the festivities were over, he said, he and Coolidge strolled around the Amherst campus. Finally, they stretched out under some shade trees. Gazing over the familiar landscape of gently rolling hills, they talked about the futures they were planning for themselves. Both wanted to become lawyers; this was one of the bonds that had helped form their friendship. Morrow, feeling adventurous, said that he was thinking of going to Pittsburgh, Pennsylvania—which, at that time, was considered a gateway to the beckoning West. He asked Coolidge, "Where do you think you will go?"

The practical, common sense Coolidge looked in the direction of Northampton, seven miles away. "Northampton is the nearest courthouse," he replied.

Chapter 4

Getting Started

Coolidge spent the summer of 1895 at home in Plymouth. He helped with chores around the farm and spent his spare time reading — that year he favored poetry, especially the works of Sir Walter Scott, Rudyard Kipling, and William Shakespeare. Colonel Coolidge had hoped that his son would stay in Plymouth and follow him in the family tradition of storekeeping and farming, but he made no objection when he learned that Calvin had other ambitions. At the end of the summer the young man went to Northampton, hoping to find a way to enter the legal profession.

BECOMING A LAWYER

At the close of the 19th century, there were two ways to become a lawyer. One way was to go to one of the many new law schools that had opened up at universities in the bigger cities. But many young men — including many former Presidents, such as Benjamin Harrison — still followed the old-fashioned way, which was to study independently in a lawyer's office. Under this system, the law student would spend about three years working as a legal clerk or assistant. During this time, he would discuss cases with an experienced lawyer, who would also assign articles and books for the clerk to read.

After such a period of combined work and study, students were usually able to pass the examination of the state legal association. This test was called the bar examination. Once a student passed it, he was qualified to practice law in that state, whether he had attended law school or not. This method had been used by aspiring lawyers since the earliest days of the American colonies, and this was the method Coolidge chose.

Calvin found a position in the Northampton law office of John C. Hammond and Henry P. Field. There, in a corner of the reception room, he was given a desk where he could perform his duties. One day he might be asked to copy out a will, a deed, or some other legal document. The next day, his task might be to look up references in law books that filled many long shelves in the office. In short, he did anything that needed to be done to help the partners conduct their business. Whenever he had a moment free, he read law books and case reports.

Winning a Prize

One day Calvin received some good news. As a senior at Amherst, he had written an essay called "The Principles Fought for in the American Revolution." He later entered the essay in a nationwide contest sponsored by a patriotic organization called the "Sons of the American Revolution." The essay won first prize in the contest—a gold medal worth $150.

Coolidge was so modest that he did not tell anyone about the prize he had won. One of his employers, Judge Henry

Field, found out about it from the newspaper. Coolidge did not tell his father about the prize, either. He admitted later that he thought it would come as a bigger surprise to the colonel if he read about it in the papers.

REPUBLICAN LAWYER

Coolidge worked and studied in the Hammond and Field law office for about 20 months. At that point he decided that he was ready to take the bar examination, although the usual period of preparation was closer to 36 months. But Coolidge determinedly took the test—and passed it. He became a Massachusetts lawyer in July 1897.

Because he had come to feel at home in Northampton, Coolidge had no desire to set himself up in legal practice elsewhere. Nor did he want to join an established firm or to take a partner. His law practice was a one-man operation from the start. This not only made it more difficult for him to attract clients, but once he had attracted them, it sometimes made it more difficult for him to do everything that needed to be done in order to keep them. But Calvin was a true "loner" who preferred to be on his own.

Coolidge rented a two-room office in downtown Northampton and used $800 that he had inherited from his mother's father to buy a good library of legal reference books and a set of office furniture. As for his personal life, he lived in an inexpensive rooming house. He had no desire for fancy meals, elegant clothing, or the trimmings of a luxurious life. As long as his meals were simple and nourishing and his clothes were respectable, he was satisfied.

Coolidge worked hard during his first three years as a lawyer—so hard that he did not take the time to visit his father and stepmother in Plymouth until 1900. But he accomplished much. He built up a small but solid legal practice, and his skill as an attorney began to be recognized. He even won a case from his former employer and teacher, John Hammond. He was invited to become the vice-president of a small local bank and also the bank's attorney. In addition to these business activities, he became involved in local politics — Republican politics, of course.

Rise in Local Politics

Soon after coming to Northampton, Coolidge joined the state Republican Party committee that represented the district in which he lived. He associated with party leaders, shared their concerns, and established a reputation among them for quiet dependability and loyalty to the party. He ran for the Northampton city council in 1899 and was elected; he was re-elected in 1900. The position did not offer a salary, but it did give Calvin a start in politics.

In 1900 Coolidge was appointed solicitor, or attorney, for the city. This position carried a salary of $600 a year and lasted for two years. In 1903, he served as clerk of the courts of Hampshire County, the county in which Northampton was located. The following year, the local Republicans elected him chairman of their party's county committee. Calvin Coolidge was beginning to be somebody in the Northampton area. Clubs and organizations started inviting him to dinners and asking him to be a speaker.

In 1905 Coolidge ran for a seat on the Northampton School Board and was defeated. This was the only time in his entire political career that he was to lose an election. But by now he was involved in Republican Party activities at the state level, and he had every reason to hope that his own political career would soon advance beyond Northampton. He believed that he was now ready to move into the larger world of state politics. Meanwhile, changes were taking place in his private life.

COURTSHIP AND MARRIAGE

One morning in 1903, Coolidge was at home in his bedroom in the boardinghouse where he lived on the edge of Northampton. He was standing in front of a mirror, shaving, and for some reason he was wearing only a suit of long underwear and a hat. Suddenly he heard a burst of laughter nearby. Turning toward the window, he saw a young woman standing across the street in front of the Clarke Institute for the Deaf. She had caught a glimpse of the strange sight of Coolidge shaving in his odd get-up, and she had been unable to keep from laughing aloud. Although he was embarrassed, he smiled at her — then closed the window and pulled the shade.

That was the first meeting between Coolidge and Grace Anne Goodhue, but it was not the last. Calvin's social life was not the liveliest in Northampton, but he did take part in activities such as canoe outings, picnics, card parties, and, occasionally, dances. Before long he began to see Grace Goodhue at these gatherings. Apparently he was attracted to her from the start.

Grace was seven years younger than Calvin, pretty and slim. Like Coolidge, she was a Vermonter, the daughter of Andrew I. Goodhue and Lemira Barrett Goodhue of Burlington, Vermont, where she had been born in 1879. She attended the University of Vermont, graduated in 1902, and came to Northampton to work as an instructor at the school for the deaf. Her job was teaching deaf children how to understand what people were saying by reading the movements of their lips.

Opposites Attract

In some ways, Coolidge and Grace were opposites. He was quiet and somewhat withdrawn. He said little, and when he did speak, his remarks were often dryly humorous or even sarcastic. Grace, on the other hand, was lively, outgoing, and very sociable. But the difference in their personalities only seemed to make them more interested in one another.

It was not long before Calvin and Grace were courting regularly. By the early summer of 1905, Coolidge had decided that this was the woman he wanted to marry. Even when proposing to the woman he loved, however, he remained a man of few words. Instead of a flowery, romantic declaration of passion, he simply declared to Grace one day: "I am going to be married to you." Fortunately, Grace understood him well enough to know that his feelings were deep and sincere, in spite of his matter-of-fact way of showing them. She accepted his proposal and the two became engaged. They planned to marry in June of 1906.

A Silent Visit

First, though, there was one high hurdle to clear. Because Grace's parents lived up north in Burlington, Coolidge did not meet them during his courtship of Grace. But once the couple announced their engagement, it was time for the prospective groom to pay the necessary "get-acquainted" visit to his fiancée's family.

The visit was not a success. Coolidge seems not to have

liked the Goodhues, and they clearly did not think much of him—possibly because they were Democrats and he was a Republican, or possibly because he spent the entire visit sitting on the end of a sofa and did not say a word until it was time to leave. His lack of social graces upset Grace's mother, who declared that he was not good enough for her daughter and tried as hard as she could to break up the relationship or at least postpone the wedding.

But, although she was very fond of her parents, Grace in her own way was as stubborn as Coolidge. She knew that Calvin was devoted to her and that he was intelligent, serious, and ambitious. She believed she had chosen a good man, and she refused to be talked out of her choice. In fact, she agreed to Coolidge's suggestion that they could end the wrangling with her mother simply by getting married ahead of schedule.

A Short Honeymoon

Much to the dismay of Mrs. Goodhue, Grace and Calvin were married on October 4, 1905. Although Grace's mother softened toward Coolidge sufficiently to allow the wedding to take place in the Goodhue home, she was not happy about it. For the rest of her life, in fact, she remained on bad terms with her son-in-law, and she always claimed that his successes were really Grace's doing.

The wedding was small, with only about 15 guests. The newlyweds had planned a two-week honeymoon in Montreal, Canada. After only one week, however, Coolidge felt that they had seen all the sights in Montreal and might as well go home and save the money that the second week would cost. Grace might have been disappointed at this change of plans, but if so, she gave no sign of it. From the first week of their marriage to the last, she showed a great deal of patience and

Coolidge's marriage to Grace Goodhue was a happy and devoted one. This picture was taken after Coolidge's retirement from the presidency. The collie dog, named Rob Roy, was one of the family's many pets. (Library of Congress.)

tact when it came to coping with Coolidge's penny-pinching, his stubbornness, and his moody silences.

So the honeymooners left Montreal and turned for home. But on the way back to Northampton, they stopped in Boston and visited the state capitol building, where the governor had his office. One room contained a large and impressive chair. It was the official state chair of the governor of Massachusetts. Playfully, the newlyweds decided to try sitting in it. To their intense embarrassment, a guard caught them in the act and shooed them away. For years afterward, they laughed sheepishly at the memory of that awkward moment. They had no way of knowing that Coolidge would some day be elected to sit in that very chair.

STATE POLITICS

Back in Northampton, the Coolidges settled into married life. Calvin wanted to remain in his old boardinghouse lodgings for a while, as it was an inexpensive way to live. But when Grace became pregnant, he knew that they needed a house of their own in which to raise a family. So, about 11 months after they were married, the Coolidges moved into their first home, a rented duplex apartment. Their first child, a boy whom they named John Coolidge, was born two weeks after the move, on September 7.

Looking back on that happy day, Coolidge later remembered the perfume of a flowering vine that grew on the wall outside the bedroom. He wrote, "The fragrance of the clematis which covered the bay window filled the room like a benediction where the mother lay with her baby. It was all very wonderful to us."

While Coolidge's family life was beginning, his political career moved ahead, too. In 1906 he ran for his first state office—and won. He was elected to the Massachusetts state legislature's house of representatives, which was called the General Court. He served in that office for two terms of one year each, from January of 1907 through the end of 1908. During this time he spent weekends at home in Northampton with Grace and little John. Each week when the legislature was in session, he took the early-morning Monday train to Boston, where he rented a room at an inexpensive hotel called the Adams House. This was the part-time home of many state legislators, the men who were Coolidge's new associates.

Coolidge's two terms as a state legislator were unremarkable. He did not call attention to himself by any special accomplishments, but he did his duties faithfully and regularly. He showed a knack for understanding how things were done in the world of politics, and he made some important friends.

One friend who would have a lasting effect on Coolidge's life and political career was Murray Crane, a former governor of Massachusetts who was one of Massachusetts' two U.S. senators. Crane was the leader of the state's Republicans. That made him the real leader of Massachusetts politics, for the Republicans were more powerful than the Democrats throughout most of the state at that time.

It appears that Crane took notice of Coolidge early in Calvin's first legislative term. The intelligence, ambition, and party loyalty of the young man from Vermont made a good impression on Crane, who described Coolidge as "one of the coming men of this country."

Progressive Ideas

Senator Murray Crane and Massachusetts legislator Calvin Coolidge shared the political beliefs that had been shaped by the most famous Republican of the day, President Theodore

Roosevelt, who occupied the White House from 1901 to 1909. Throughout his political career and his rise to the presidency, Roosevelt had promoted ideas that were called "progressive." These progressive ideas included such notions as laws to protect laborers from unsafe working conditions and laws to limit the power of large corporations. Another progressive idea was that women should have the right to vote.

During his two years in the Massachusetts legislature, Coolidge supported these ideals of the progressive wing of the Republican Party. Many of the laws that were proposed and discussed in the legislature had to do with working conditions and hours. At that time, many communities had no laws to control the demands that employers could make of their employees. For example, many factory workers had to work seven days a week or lose their jobs. Coolidge voted in favor of a law that would limit the workweek to six days.

Another important issue of the time was child labor. In the industrial cities of the East Coast, including Boston, many women and children of the poorer classes were employed in crowded, unsanitary factories that were sometimes called "sweatshops." Even very young children sometimes worked 12-hour or 14-hour days, often doing jobs that damaged their health, such as sewing in poor light, which cost many children their eyesight. As a progressive, Coolidge voted in support of laws to improve hazardous job conditions and to limit the number of hours that children could work.

Another progressive cause concerned the direct election of U.S. senators. Ever since the early days of the American republic, congressmen—that is, members of the U.S. House of Representatives—had been elected by the direct vote of the people in their districts. Members of the U.S. Senate, however, arrived there by different routes. In some states, the senators were appointed by the governor. In other states, they were elected by the people. In most states, however, U.S. senators were elected by the members of the state legislature, who in turn had been elected by the people.

The progressive members of the Republican Party, as well as some Democrats, wanted U.S. senators to be elected directly by the people in every state, just as congressmen were. Coolidge voted in favor of changing the Massachusetts state constitution to bring about the direct election of U.S. senators. (From 1913 on, U.S. senators from all states have been chosen by direct election.)

BACK TO NORTHAMPTON

Coolidge chose not to run for a third term in the Massachusetts legislature. Although he felt that he had gained valuable political experience, he did not believe that serving additional years in the Massachusetts General Court would help advance his career in politics. Furthermore, his salary as a legislator was not very high, and his legislative duties required him to spend a great deal of time in Boston. This kept him away from his small, one-man law practice, which, as a result, did not bring in much additional income.

And the Coolidge family was growing. A second child, a boy named Calvin Coolidge, Jr., was born on April 13, 1908. More than ever before, Coolidge felt the need to earn a good, steady living. So, at the end of 1908, he returned to Northampton and spent a year building up his law practice.

A Conscientious Mayor

This did not mean that Coolidge turned his back on politics. Far from it — in fact, he was more active than ever in Republican Party affairs. In 1910 the city Republican committee urged him to run for mayor of Northampton. He did so, and was easily elected over his Democratic opponent, Harry Bicknell. In 1911, Bicknell again ran against Coolidge, and Coolidge won a second mayoral term.

Coolidge was proud of his service to the city he had made his home. Many years later, in his autobiography, he wrote, "Of all the honors that have come to me, I still cherish in a very high place the confidence of my friends and neighbors in making me their mayor." He celebrated his win in the first mayoral election by going to Montpelier, Vermont, to visit his father, who was serving a term in the Vermont state legislature.

Coolidge's personal characteristics of thrift and simplicity were reflected in the job he did as mayor. When he came to office, the city of Northampton was in debt. After two years under Coolidge's guidance, the city had paid off much of its debt, even though its income was reduced because he had also managed to lower the taxes paid by Northampton residents. At the same time, valuable civic services were performed, too: the police and fire departments were enlarged, and the streets and sidewalks were repaved and improved.

Overall, Coolidge was a conscientious mayor who performed his public duties faithfully. Unlike many elected officials at all levels of government, he did not allow his position to become an excuse for expensive habits, a showy lifestyle, or a self-important attitude.

In 1911, while Coolidge was still serving his second term as mayor of Northampton, the Republican Party was helping to shape his future. As the end of his mayoral term approached, the county Republican committee asked him to run for the state senate. This would mean returning to state politics in Boston, but it would be a bit different than his earlier service in the General Court. Of the two houses in the Massachusetts state legislature, the state senate was smaller but more powerful than the General Court. State senators actually planned and wrote the bills that eventually became law, while the representatives merely voted on them. The state senate was generally considered to be a better springboard to higher political office. Coolidge did not want to be mayor forever, and he had learned that he did not really want to settle down into a small-town law practice. So he agreed to run for the Massachusetts senate in 1912.

Chapter 5

To the Governor's Chair

Friends warned Coolidge that winning election to the state senate would not be easy. His senatorial district included Northampton, which had many Republican voters who would be happy to send Coolidge to the senate. But the district also included a large area outside Northampton, where many Democrats lived. However, when his advisors predicted that the race would be difficult, Coolidge calmly replied, "Well, it will be just as difficult for the other fellow."

And he was right. When it was time to go to the polls, the Northampton voters were solidly behind Coolidge, and they carried the day. Coolidge was elected. After two years as mayor of Northampton, he set off once again for Boston, this time to serve in the state senate.

A THRIFTY LIFE-STYLE

In Boston, Coolidge took up residence once again in the Adams House, where he had lived during the two years he was in the General Court. He went back there partly because

44

it was easier than finding somewhere new to live, but mostly because it was so cheap—only $1.50 a day.

Although he was now 40 years old and an established lawyer and politician, Coolidge was just as careful with money as he had ever been. The Coolidge family home in Northampton was a small, rented, duplex apartment. John and Calvin, Jr., attended public school instead of a private school, which would have been much more expensive. And, unlike many middle-class housewives of the time, Grace did not have a full-time servant or maid. She did much of the housework herself, helped out by a hired girl who came in for the day from time to time. On Mondays, Grace even washed the family laundry, something that few lawyers' wives would have been expected to do themselves, and pinned it to a clothesline in the yard to dry.

The Coolidges lived in this thrifty way for several reasons. One was that Coolidge simply hated to spend money unless he absolutely had to. He believed in hard work and simple living, and he liked to add to his savings rather than spend his money on unnecessary luxuries.

Automobiles, for example, were becoming popular in Northampton, and one of Coolidge's friends, a man named Fred Jager, became the town's first automobile dealer. Jager tried for years to persuade Coolidge to buy a car, but Coolidge never did. When Jager came around offering to take Coolidge out for a "test ride" in a new automobile, Coolidge always turned him down. Then he would politely add, "But Grace would be glad to go." So Jager would end up taking Grace for a ride, which she enjoyed immensely, but the dealer knew full well that it was Coolidge, not his wife, who controlled the family pocketbook.

Coolidge held onto his money because he desperately wanted to remain independent and self-sufficient. One of his greatest fears was of falling into debt. He once told Jim Lucey, a Northampton shoemaker who had been a friend since Coolidge's Amherst days, that he could sleep better at night knowing that he did not owe anything to anyone.

Another reason for Coolidge's thrifty life-style was his income. Although he was a diligent lawyer, his true ambition and dedication were directed toward politics, not the law. He did not attract many new clients to his legal practice, and he spent long periods away from his law office on political business. As a result, the income from his legal practice remained modest, although it provided a comfortable living. Furthermore, his early political posts, as a member of the Massachusetts state legislature and as mayor of Northampton, did not carry very high salaries. So the Coolidges were careful with their money, and Grace cheerfully adopted her husband's penny-pinching ways and managed the household on a small budget.

STATE SENATOR

In all, Coolidge served in the Massachusetts state senate for four terms of one year each, from 1912 through 1915. He continued to share the goals and beliefs of the Republican Party and could always be counted on to support the party's position in local and national affairs. During his first year in office, Republican President William Howard Taft ran for re-election, and Coolidge campaigned for him, making speeches throughout the Northampton area. Unfortunately for the Republicans, Taft was defeated by Woodrow Wilson, the Democratic candidate.

On the senate floor, Coolidge supported many of the causes for which he had voted as a state legislator several years earlier, including the right to vote for women, minimum wages for women workers, worker's compensation (payments to employees who are injured on the job and cannot work), and the direct election of U.S. senators.

Settling a Strike

First-year senators are not usually given important roles to play in state affairs, but Coolidge happened to be assigned to a prominent position during his very first term in the state senate. Lawrence, Massachusetts, was the site of a number of textile mills—factories where cloth was made from raw materials such as cotton and wool. In 1912, laborers at the mills went on strike, refusing to return to work until they were given safer and more sanitary working conditions, shorter hours, and higher wages. The mill owners refused to agree to these demands. The striking laborers then threatened to destroy the mills if the owners tried to hire new workers.

The strike crippled the Massachusetts economy and included some incidents of rock-throwing and protest marches that frightened the middle-class majority of the Lawrence townspeople. Something had to be done to bring the confrontation to an end, so the state legislature named several of its members to a special Conciliation Committee to work out an agreement between the laborers on the one hand and the mill owners and managers on the other.

Coolidge was named chairman of this committee, which meant that the task of settling the dispute was essentially up to him. His success in this difficult task shows his real integrity as a statesman. Although he could have won the support (and the votes) of either labor or management by siding with one group over the other, that was not his way. He felt that neither side was totally right or wrong.

The strike of the Lawrence, Massachusetts, textile workers received nationwide attention. Here, children of the striking workers are shown on a protest march through New York City. (Library of Congress.)

Instead of taking sides, Coolidge persuaded the laborers to give up a few of their demands. He also persuaded the owners to give in to a few of the labor demands. Thus he brought the two sides together and settled the strike. Neither side was completely happy with the results, and Coolidge realized that he was not going to be wildly popular with either group of voters. But he did win public approval for putting an end to a dangerous and disruptive problem.

The American Labor Movement

The strike at the Lawrence textile mills that Coolidge settled during his first term in the Massachusetts state senate was one of many strikes that ruffled the waters of American business in the early years of the 20th century. The strikes were part of the growing American labor movement, in which workers united to form associations called unions. A union could speak or act on behalf of all of its members and could wield more influence than the individual workers could hope to do. Unions became increasingly powerful during the years of Calvin Coolidge's political rise.

The first American unions dated from the early days of the republic, in the final years of the 18th century, when craftsmen of certain guilds, such as carpenters or shoemakers, joined together to form citywide federations. Beginning in the 1830s, efforts were started to join these local federations into nationwide labor organizations. The nation's printers formed the first such union in 1850.

The union movement continued to grow, as workers in various trades discovered that union action helped them obtain benefits from factory owners and managers who were concerned only with making the highest possible profits. Sometimes the unions operated at the edge of the law, or even outside it, as in the case of a secret workers' organization in the coal-mining region of Pennsylvania. This labor group was called the Molly Maguires. Its stated purpose was to combat the abuse of miners by the mine owners, but its actions were those of terrorists—threats, beatings, bombings, and even murder. The Molly Maguires disbanded when their leaders were jailed, but their actions caused many Americans to fear the very idea of labor unions.

In the 1880s, national labor unions that combined many trades emerged. The first of these was the Knights of Labor, which had more than one million members across the country by 1886. After that year, the Knights of Labor union was overshadowed by a new organization that ultimately became the largest and most powerful labor union in the land. It was founded by Samuel Gompers and was called the American Federation of Labor, or AFL.

The goals of the AFL were to help union members obtain better pay and working conditions (usually through strikes) and to support political candidates who supported the labor movement. Many other trade unions joined the AFL over the years, including the Committee for Industrial Organization (CIO) in 1955. Today, known as the AFL–CIO, the union formed by Gompers in the 19th century remains the largest in the United States.

In Coolidge's time, the labor movement provoked strong reactions from both the laboring class and the upper class. Workers felt that unions were vitally needed to protect their basic rights, to help them earn a decent living, and to give them a way to confront the powerful factory owners. Those who owned and managed the nation's factories, mines, and railroads, on the other hand, pointed out that the unions often used violence and intimidation to achieve their goals, and that many union leaders made enormous profits on the dues paid by the union members.

Today, as in Coolidge's time, the country's labor unions are a focus for strong feelings of support or opposition—and a force to be reckoned with in American politics.

The Western Trolley Act

Another of Coolidge's triumphs as a state senator was his handling of a controversial bill called the Western Trolley Act. It came before the state legislature in 1913, during Coolidge's second term, at a time when he was acting as the chairman of the senate's Committee on Railroads. If it became law, this act would allow the New Haven Railroad Company to build a network of trolley lines to connect Northampton and other small towns of western Massachusetts with each other, as well as with Boston and the larger towns of the east.

Many people opposed the Western Trolley Act because they felt that the New Haven Railroad was already too large and too wealthy, and they did not want to increase its power or its profits. But Coolidge supported the act because he believed that the towns of western Massachusetts were too isolated. The dairy farmers and other small businessmen of his district would benefit from being able to ship their products to one another more easily.

Coolidge therefore encouraged his fellow senators to support the Western Trolley Act. He was so successful that the bill was passed and made into law, even though the governor, who was a Democrat, opposed it. Coolidge was proud of his victory in the long, drawn-out, and heated tussle over the Western Trolley Act and later remarked, "That was the most enjoyable session I ever spent with any legislative body."

"Have Faith in Massachusetts"

Coolidge's fellow senators respected his honesty and fair-mindedness. They elected him to the post of president of the state senate during his third and fourth terms, in 1914 and 1915. When he first took office as president of the senate, in 1914, he was called upon to deliver a speech. It was not a long speech or a flowery, elaborate, or exciting one, but it drew upon the straightforward speaking skills that Coolidge had sharpened in his school debates.

The speech set forth some of Coolidge's fundamental ideas about society: for example, that work was the basis of all organized societies, that people should not expect government programs to eliminate the need to work, and that the government should not interfere too much in the management of the economy—in other words, that people and corporations should be left alone to make money as best they could, and social progress for all would follow.

Coolidge's speech appealed to his upper- and middle-class fellow senators. When it was published, it also appealed to the middle-class majority of his fellow citizens. It was printed and reprinted many times under the title "Have Faith in Massachusetts." Coolidge remained proud of it throughout his career and always claimed that it was the best speech he ever made.

THE GREAT WAR

Far beyond the boundaries of Massachusetts, the world was being shaken by great events during Coolidge's years as president of the state senate. In August of 1914, war broke out in Europe, and soon nearly all the nations of the Western World were embroiled in a titanic conflict on European and Middle Eastern soil.

At the time, this conflict was called the Great War; today we know it as World War I. The opponents consisted of two groups of nations that were linked together by alliances and treaties: France, Great Britain, and Russia were on one side; Germany, Turkey, and Austria-Hungary were on the other.

Under Democratic President Woodrow Wilson (who held office from 1913 to 1921), the United States stayed out of the war for several years. Although most Americans were sympathetic to the British and French and were cheering for these allies to defeat Germany, the majority of the American people agreed with Wilson that the United States should not become involved in a European conflict.

Public opinion changed, however, when Germany's aggressive war at sea, especially its submarine attacks on the ships of nations that were not at war, began claiming large numbers of American lives. Americans then displayed a more warlike spirit, and finally Congress declared war on Germany on April 6, 1917. By this time, the British and French armies were somewhat weakened by the massive death tolls they had experienced, so the two million U.S. soldiers who were sent to the battlefields of France probably turned the tide of war against the Germans.

Fighting ended in November of 1918, with the United States, France, Great Britain, and Russia as the victors. After the war, President Wilson became one of the principal organizers of an international association that was formed. Called the League of Nations, it was the forerunner of today's United Nations. Wilson hoped that the League would help preserve world peace, and he was eager for the United States to become a member. Congress, however, voted against joining the League, feeling that the United States should stand on its own rather than become involved in international conflicts.

The turmoil of the war years had little direct effect on Coolidge. He was too old to be drafted for military service, and his sons, of course, were too young. So he continued to serve his country in Massachusetts. When war broke out in Europe, he was president of the state senate. But by the time the United States entered the war in 1917, he had been elected to a new office.

FIRST STATEWIDE VICTORY

In 1915, the Republicans of Massachusetts went to the polls to vote for their party's candidates for governor and lieutenant governor. The candidate they chose to run for governor was Samuel McCall, a popular U.S. congressman. Their candidate for lieutenant governor was Calvin Coolidge. It was the first time his name had appeared on a ballot for a statewide election. On election day, McCall and Coolidge defeated their Democratic opponents to become the new top officials of the state.

As lieutenant governor, Coolidge occupied a position similar to that of the Vice-President of the United States. It was his responsibility to be ready to take over the state administration if anything happened to the governor. He also had a considerable voice in making appointments (that is, in selecting people for state jobs and honors) and in issuing pardons (to criminals who were being reprieved from the death penalty, for example). In addition, Coolidge served as the head of a committee to improve Boston's elevated railway and streetcar system.

Family Life

Although his office and his duties were in Boston, Coolidge remained a resident of Northampton. He continued to take the train into Boston every Monday morning, just as he had done during his years in the state legislature. Now that he was lieutenant governor, he often brought Grace with him to attend some official function, and occasionally he brought the boys, when they were not in school.

The Coolidges' family life remained as ordinary and homespun as it had always been. On Sundays the family attended Edwards Congregational Church in Northampton. Grace continued to do most of the housework. The boys did chores around the house. They also did odd jobs for neighbors, and they divided their earnings between savings and donations to the church.

Coolidge himself enjoyed the simple pleasures of life. His one vice was smoking cigars. He drank very little, but he enjoyed fishing, taking walks, and window shopping. He also saw nothing wrong with helping Grace cook dinner or wash the dishes—behavior that one reporter noted was most uncommon for a man at that time, especially for a lieutenant governor.

Building a Base of Support

As lieutenant governor, Coolidge had the opportunity to become known to voters outside his town and his district. Governor McCall received many invitations to make speeches, attend dinners, or present awards. Because he could not accept all the invitations he received, McCall turned a number of these tasks over to his lieutenant governor. Coolidge used them to build up a base of support around the state, frequently delivering his "Have Faith in Massachusetts" speech to great applause.

Coolidge also campaigned around the state on behalf of the Republican presidential candidate of 1916, Charles Evans Hughes (who was defeated by Wilson). And he made speeches in support of the war effort—for example, urging his listeners to buy savings bonds that would help pay the army's expenses. The result of all this activity was that after three years as lieutenant governor, from 1916 through 1918, Coolidge was well known throughout Massachusetts.

WINNING THE GOVERNORSHIP

In 1918 Governor McCall decided not to run for re-election. When the Massachusetts Republicans asked themselves who was to run in McCall's place, the answer was obvious: Calvin Coolidge. The lieutenant governor was therefore nominated to run for the governorship.

The election race against Democrat Richard I. Long was very close. The Democratic Party was strong in 1918 because the United States was winning the war under the leadership of a Democratic President. But Coolidge defeated Long by a small margin.

Coolidge was sworn into office in January of 1919—in the same state capitol building where he and Grace had once been shooed out of the governor's chair by an irate guard. She stood next to him at the swearing-in ceremony, and perhaps she smiled at the memory. John and Calvin, Jr., were there, too, and Colonel Coolidge came down from Plymouth.

After the ceremony, the Coolidge family gathered around the newly elected governor in his private office. He sat in the chair, looked around him, and then said to his wife with the New England twang that never left his voice, "Well, I guess they won't turn us out this time."

Chapter 6

The Vice-Presidency

T he inauguration of Governor Coolidge was a formal event, attended by all Massachusetts dignitaries and filled with ceremony and tradition. But as soon as it was over, Coolidge settled down to the business of being governor in the same plain and simple manner he had always followed. Instead of moving into a fancy home and calling it a "governor's mansion," as was the custom in many states, he continued to live in his old room at the Adams Hotel in Boston.

Because of the increased importance of his position, however, Coolidge did ask the management to rent him the next room, so that now he had two hotel rooms as his executive residence, for a total of $2.50 a day. During the day, he worked in his office at the state capitol building, and on weekends he returned to his home and family in Northampton, if he could.

AN EFFECTIVE GOVERNOR

Coolidge's first official act as governor was to agree to the Massachusetts legislature's plan to spend $10,000 on a welcome-home celebration for soldiers from the New England states who were returning from the battlefronts of Europe. The Yankee Division landed in Boston Harbor in April 1919 and marched in a parade along Commonwealth Avenue. It

During his governorship, Coolidge left Boston for Northampton as often as possible to spend time with Grace and their two sons, Calvin, Jr. (left) and John. (Library of Congress.)

took five hours for the entire division to pass a reviewing stand where the governors of Maine, New Hampshire, Vermont, Rhode Island, and Connecticut stood next to Coolidge.

This occasion gave rise to one of the stories about "Silent Cal" that was repeated for years afterward. It seems that Coolidge stood next to Governor John H. Bartlett of New Hampshire. After saying a brief hello to Bartlett, Coolidge turned to watch the parade, and he kept on watching it for hours. It was a cold, blustery day, and the viewers soon grew stiff and uncomfortable. Finally, Coolidge turned to Bartlett and suggested politely that Bartlett might be more comfortable if he leaned on a nearby rail. Then he returned to watching the passing soldiers. Later, Bartlett marveled, "I cannot comprehend a man who could stand five hours and have nothing else to say!"

The Boston Police Strike

It is often the case with those in high office that one dramatic event captures the people's imaginations and remains in their memories. In Coolidge's case, that event was the Boston police strike in September 1919, his ninth month in office. Forever after, the Boston police strike has been remembered by historians and by the American people in general as the outstanding event of Coolidge's governorship.

Certainly the police strike was a dramatic and important occurrence. It illustrated the growing conflict in American society between workers seeking the right to strike and those who felt that strikes were wrong. It also gave Coolidge the chance to demonstrate his qualities of patience, coolness, and firmness—not just to the state that had elected him to office, but to the whole country.

The strike had another important effect as well. At that time, governors of Massachusetts were elected for one year only (they now serve four-year terms), and the election was scheduled for the fall, just after the strike was settled. Because of the decisive way in which he had restored the rule of law and order during the strike, Coolidge had no trouble being re-elected for a second term. Once again, his opponent was Richard Long of Framingham, but this time he beat Long by a good margin, even though he could not campaign because he was sick in bed with influenza.

Laws Enacted

Although Coolidge's other activities as governor were overshadowed by the Boston police strike, he did accomplish some noteworthy things during his two years in office. He continued to support some of the progressive ideas that he had favored earlier in his political career. Under his guidance, a law was passed to limit the workweek of women and children to 48 hours. He also passed a law regulating outdoor advertising;

this law made Massachusetts one of the first states in which the number and size of billboards and signposts were limited by law.

Coolidge even applied his lifelong habit of saving and budgeting his own money to the state's financial problems. He created a statewide budget system for the first time in the state's history. This meant that the state's income from taxes, as well as its spending on public projects and services, would now be kept track of by a central accounting office. Such a system brought considerable savings to the state.

REORGANIZING THE STATE

One thing that troubled Coolidge during his governorship was the question of appointments to public jobs. He soon learned that any political leader who is in a position to award jobs or other benefits is constantly sought after by people who hope to influence him or to gain his favor. It was expected that, when Coolidge had jobs or honors to award, he would favor Republicans who had supported him in the past, and he did so.

However, Coolidge refused to be influenced by friends or supporters of job-seekers, because he liked to make up his own mind and hated to be dictated to. Furthermore, unlike many politicians of that and other times, he never accepted money or favors from anyone, Republican or Democrat, because he could not bear to be thought anything other than completely honest.

A Distasteful Task

Just before Coolidge took office as governor, the Massachusetts state legislature had voted to amend, or change, the state constitution. The changes made would simplify and streamline the organization of the state government and administration. The biggest effect of the change was that 144 separate departments of the state administration were to be combined into only 20.

This change would save the state a great deal of money, because it would eliminate many state employees who would no longer be needed. But it also meant that Coolidge had to choose the 20 department heads, out of 144, who would keep their jobs in the new organization. In other words, he had to fire 124 men who had achieved high-ranking positions in the state administration and were proud of both their prestige and their handsome salaries. Of course, the competition for the remaining jobs was fierce, and the department heads and their friends besieged Coolidge night and day.

For weeks Coolidge agonized over this distasteful task. He refused to discuss the 20 appointments with anyone, preferring to make up his own mind. Finally, he got up from his desk one day with the completed list in his hand and said to his secretary, "I am glad it is done. It was the worst job I have ever had to do. I hope I shall never have to do anything like that again." Coolidge had his list read aloud at once to the state senate, which approved of his choices. The officials who were rejected were naturally downcast and bitter, but Coolidge simply pointed out that he had done his best.

Several years later, a friend remarked to Coolidge that it had taken a lot of courage to step in and settle the Boston police strike. Coolidge replied that the Boston police strike had called for "a little" courage, but that reorganizing the state administration had been his most difficult and most courageous act, because he wanted to do it right even at the cost of making many powerful enemies.

THE ELECTION OF 1920

In June of 1920, during Coolidge's second year as governor of Massachusetts, members of the national committee of the Republican Party gathered in Chicago. It was a presidential election year, and the purpose of the Republican convention was to elect the party's candidate for President and also the candidate for Vice-President. Coolidge did not attend the convention, but it was a turning point in his life and career nonetheless.

The Reluctant Candidate

Coolidge's success in quelling the Boston police strike brought him national attention, and there were some people—especially in Massachusetts—who felt that he should run for President in 1920. One of Coolidge's closest friends and staunchest supporters was a man named Frank Stearns, a leading officer in the Republican Party of Massachusetts. Stearns had befriended Coolidge during Coolidge's period in the state legislature, and he had often predicted that Coolidge might sit in the White House some day.

In early 1920, Stearns organized a Coolidge for President Committee and even opened a campaign office in Washington, D.C. But this was done without the permission of Coolidge, who did not approve. He ordered Stearns to disband the committee and to end all talk of Coolidge for President in 1920. Furthermore, he refused to discuss the possibility of becoming President with his supporters in the party or even with friends.

Several reasons have been offered to explain Coolidge's reluctance to run for President in 1920. According to Coolidge himself, he was satisfied just to be governor of Massachusetts. He said several times that the governorship was more than he had ever hoped to achieve, and that he had no desire to look higher. But many politicians have been known to be modest about their ambitions, so it is quite possible that Coolidge did hope to be President one day.

Above all things, however, Coolidge was hardheaded and realistic. He knew it was very unlikely that he would be able to win the Republican Party's nomination as its presidential candidate in 1920, because he simply did not have enough support from around the nation to defeat the other potential candidates. And he was shrewd enough to realize that it would be better for him to wait for a later opportunity than to try at once and fail. Therefore, Coolidge did not listen to those who advised him to try for the presidency. He just waited in Boston to hear who was chosen by the delegates at the Chicago convention.

A Deadlocked Convention

The two most favored candidates to receive the party's nomination for President were Governor Frank O. Lowden of Illinois and General Leonard Wood, a longtime Army officer who was popular in the western states. But when the first ballot was cast by the convention delegates, neither of these two men received a majority of votes. (Coolidge received 34 votes on that first ballot. Most of them were cast by delegates from Massachusetts in a spirit of patriotic enthusiasm for their state.)

Two more ballots were cast, but again, neither produced a majority winner. Finally, it became clear that the delegates were deadlocked and could not agree on a candidate. Senator Henry Lodge of Massachusetts, the chairman of the convention, adjourned the proceedings for the night.

A Compromise Candidate

That night, a number of powerful Republican senators met in a room of the Blackstone Hotel to smoke cigars and discuss the situation. They agreed that neither Wood nor Lowden seemed to be acceptable to enough candidates to win the nomination. They also agreed that no one wanted a long, drawn-out contest between the two that would only split the party into bitterly quarreling factions. In many conversations during the course of that night, various senators and other Republican leaders began to suggest that a third possibility, Senator Warren G. Harding of Ohio, might be able to draw enough votes to unify the party behind him.

Although there was no formal pact, Lodge and other party leaders more or less agreed to give the convention delegates four more ballots to see whether they could agree on Wood or Lowden. If not, it was understood that they would then advise all the delegates they knew to vote for Harding. This night's work gave rise to the saying that America's leaders are really chosen by a handful of behind-the-scenes plotters in "smoke-filled rooms."

On the following day, events in the convention hall went much as the Republican Party leaders had expected. Neither Wood nor Lowden could gain ground in the course of several ballots. Yet Harding, who had ended the previous day with 39 votes, jumped to 58, then to 78. Groups of delegates from Texas, Missouri, and other states began shifting their votes to him, and the more votes he acquired, the more he drew, so that his total increased steadily.

By the eighth ballot, Wood and Lowden had each dropped a considerable number of votes, and Harding was up to 133. Delegates from Ohio, tremendously excited by the surge that was carrying their senator forward, started a chanting, banner-waving demonstration for Harding on the convention floor.

By the ninth ballot, Harding led the pack with 374 votes. And the tenth and final ballot showed that the delegates knew which way the wind was blowing. Harding finished with a large majority of 692 votes. (Four die-hard Coolidge supporters from Massachusetts and one from New York voted for Coolidge all the way to this ballot.)

Chairman Lodge then invited the delegates to declare

their unanimous support for Harding—that is, to announce that he was chosen by the entire convention. A roar of applause greeted the suggestion, and Warren G. Harding was declared the party's unanimous choice for President. Now only one piece of business remained for the delegates, and that was choosing a candidate for Vice-President.

The Delegates Rebel

The men who had met at the Blackstone Hotel the night before to select Harding as their party's presidential candidate had not overlooked the need to give him a suitable running mate. They had decided that Senator Irvine Lenroot of Wisconsin would fit the bill. The party leaders were so sure that Lenroot would be chosen that, once Harding's nomination was secure, most of them left the convention floor, and so did many of the delegates—they thought the excitement was over.

Senator Medill McCormick of Illinois nominated Lenroot for the vice-presidency. The men who had first backed Harding and selected Lenroot as his running mate expected that the remaining delegates would vote in favor of Lenroot's nomination and that would be that. But something completely unexpected happened.

Most of the delegates to the convention were low-ranking members of the Republican Party. Many of them were aware that the presidential nomination had gone to Harding because of the maneuvers of a few powerful men behind the scenes, and they resented this. So they rebelled against the party leaders.

A delegate from Oregon jumped onto a chair and shouted out that he nominated Calvin Coolidge for Vice-President. Delegates applauded, and representatives from Michigan, Maryland, and half a dozen other states echoed the call for Coolidge. In one ballot, Coolidge received 674 votes; Lenroot received only 146.

Back in Boston, Coolidge and Grace waited in the governor's rooms in the Adams Hotel. They had been following the events at the convention by means of frequent telephone calls from friends in telegraph and newspaper offices in Chicago. They knew that Harding had been nominated and that Lenroot was expected to follow. Just as they were about to leave for dinner, the phone rang. Coolidge answered it, listened for a moment, and then looked at his wife and spoke a single word: "Nominated."

At age 47, after 20 years in politics, Calvin Coolidge was going to run for his first national office, but it was not his way to show his feelings. If he felt excitement, or jubilation, or worry, he kept it to himself. He merely sat in his room and quietly smoked cigars while friends and supporters thronged to the hotel to congratulate him.

VICTORY AT THE POLLS

Harding and Coolidge had been nominated by their party. Now they had to be elected at the polls in November. So the months between the convention and the election were occupied with campaign speeches and appearances designed to secure votes for the Republican team.

Coolidge did some campaigning, mostly in New England and the South. But the party knew that Harding was the speaker that audiences really wanted to hear, so Coolidge was left on his own for much of the summer after the convention. He returned to Amherst to attend the 25th reunion of his graduating class, and he was pleased to be greeted with loud applause on his arrival at his old college.

Coolidge also took his wife and sons north to Plymouth for a celebration called Old Home Week, during which Vermonters who had moved away from the town returned to visit friends and family members. The Coolidges were the most popular and sought-after of all the guests in Plymouth that week.

But the months between the convention and the election also brought sadness to Coolidge. His longtime friend and political advisor, Senator Murray Crane, died in October. Coolidge attended his funeral, deeply moved. When a newspaper photographer approached him for a picture at the graveside, Coolidge said gruffly, "I came to bury my friend. It is no time for photographs."

Coolidge *was* a vice-presidential candidate, and perhaps some of his fellow Republicans might have wanted him to be more eager for publicity. But Coolidge's dignity and his sense of what was right would not let him take advantage of such a sorrowful occasion just to get his picture in the newspapers.

Election day brought the Republicans a landslide of votes. Americans seemed to be tired of the Democrats, and many felt that the Republicans would guide them into a new era of prosperity and growth now that the Great War was behind them. Harding and Coolidge won 404 votes in the electoral college, while the Democratic team of James M. Cox and Franklin D. Roosevelt won only 127 votes. Warren G. Harding would be the 29th President of the United States, and Calvin Coolidge would be his Vice-President.

Quiet Farewells

Coolidge served his last day as governor of Massachusetts in January of 1921. On that day, he carefully tidied his desk, placed the desktop photograph of his mother in his pocket so that he could put it on his new desk, and left his office at the statehouse. He returned to Northampton for a few weeks with his family before his inauguration as Vice-President on March 4.

Women's Suffrage

As a member of the Massachusetts state legislature, Calvin Coolidge had supported the idea of women's suffrage—that is, of giving women the right to vote. Perhaps, therefore, he was especially pleased that the election of 1920, in which he was made Vice-President, was the first one in which American women were able to vote.

The question of women's suffrage had been debated in the United States ever since the days of the Constitutional Congress of 1787, when the U.S. Constitution was written. Although many early Americans argued hotly that women should be given equal voting rights with men, many others disagreed. As a result, when the Constitution was completed, it left the issue of suffrage up to the individual states—and none of the states gave women the right to vote.

During the 19th century, various women led the movement to win voting rights for women. Among them were Lucretia Mott and Elizabeth Cady Stanton, who braved the disapproval of society to organize the first women's rights meeting in history. It took place in 1848. That two-day meeting is regarded as the beginning of the women's rights movement in the United States. Because Mott, Stanton, and their followers demanded suffrage (voting rights), they came to be called "suffragettes." Today, they are more often called suffragists.

The most important of all the suffragists

These suffragists, shown during a parade at the White House in 1917, were part of a national movement that worked for more than 70 years to win the right to vote for women. Three years after this picture was taken, American women voted in a national election for the first time. (National Archives.)

was probably Susan B. Anthony, who met Stanton in 1851. The two women formed a friendship that lasted for 50 years while they fought together for women's rights. As they spoke up in the newspapers and meeting halls of the land, more and more people agreed that there was no justification for withholding the right to vote from an American citizen just because she happened to be female.

In the early years of the 20th century, many states granted women partial voting rights. For example, in some states women were allowed to vote in city or state elections but not in presidential ones; in other states, women could vote to elect members of the electoral college but could not vote in party primary elections.

The suffragists, who had formed a number of organizations with thousands of members, continued to urge that all American women be given full and equal suffrage by an amendment to the Constitution. This was done in June of 1919, when Congress passed the 19th Amendment, which says that "The right of citizens of the United States to vote shall not be denied or abridged by the United States or by any State on account of sex." The legislatures of 36 states ratified the amendment (accepted it as law) and made it an official part of the national Constitution on August 26, 1920—in time for women to vote in their first presidential election.

During those weeks, he made a point of visiting all of his Northampton friends and acquaintances and saying farewell. Yet even Coolidge's farewells were quiet affairs, not emotional ones. Jim Lucey, the shoemaker who had been a friend of Coolidge's for almost 30 years, remembered that Coolidge stood in the doorway of his shop and said, in his twanging Yankee voice, "Well, I've come to say goodbye." The two men shook hands, and Lucey knew that genuine affection lay beneath those few words. Then Coolidge left the shop. Soon after, he left Northampton for Washington, D.C., and the vice-presidency.

Chapter 7

The Harding Heritage

On a cool, sunny March 4, 1921, the new President, Warren G. Harding, and his Vice-President, Calvin Coolidge, were inaugurated (formally sworn into office). After a parade down Washington's streets, Coolidge performed his first task as Vice-President. He made a brief inaugural speech to the Senate. One of his official duties in the coming months would be to preside over the Senate. (The Vice-President is traditionally responsible for the administrative management of the Senate, although he does not vote on legislative issues unless his vote is needed to break a tie.)

The Coolidges then settled down to life in the nation's capital. They planned to continue their simple Northampton life-style, living in a small rented house and sending John and Calvin, Jr., to public school. But when they discovered that Washington rentals were considerably higher than those they were used to, Coolidge decided that his salary was not large enough to afford to rent a house. And although he had about $25,000 in a bank, he never considered dipping into his savings to pay daily living expenses.

Even as his country's second-highest public official, Coolidge felt that he must live within his income – and even save a little, if he could. So the Coolidges settled into a rental apartment in a hotel called the New Willard. It was less costly than a rented house, but it was much more fashionable and elegant than Boston's shabby old Adams House.

NEW RESPONSIBILITIES

The job of the Vice-President of the United States is not to everyone's taste. The Vice-President's principal responsibility is to stand ready to take over the presidency if the President becomes unable to carry out his duties. This means that the most important part of what the Vice-President does consists of doing nothing, just being ready.

In practice, of course, Vice-Presidents can be very active. They are the presiding officers of the Senate, which means that they oversee the proceedings on the Senate floor, but they have no legislative power there. They also represent the President and the country at all sorts of events, from state funerals to dinner parties, that the President does not attend. But many Vice-Presidents — starting with John Adams, the first person to hold that office — have complained that the job did not keep them busy enough and had no real purpose or power.

It is not known whether Coolidge shared these feelings, but if he did, he never expressed them. He simply went about his official duties in his usual quiet, efficient manner. As presiding officer of the Senate, he made sure that strict attention was paid to the parliamentary rules of order (the body of rules that governs formal meetings — for example, the rule that states that someone who wishes to speak must be recognized, or given permission to speak, by the chairman). But he took little part in the actual business of the Senate. In the same way, he received many social invitations because of his new status, and most of them could not be turned down.

Socializing was an obligation of Coolidge's position, and

he became quite used to dining out at stylish dinner parties with important people. But his essential character never changed. He did not drink, he did not care greatly about fine food, and he never learned how to make small talk. Washington's fashionable hostesses liked to have him at their parties, for he was the Vice-President, after all, but they soon learned to expect little of him. He would sit calmly at his place, nibbling on nuts and crackers, while Grace chatted and charmed the other guests.

A Cool Relationship

As for his relationship with President Harding, it was not a close one. Harding was a jovial, talkative, easy-going man with whom Coolidge had almost nothing in common. Furthermore, Coolidge disapproved of Harding's personal habits and his way of life. Harding invited his friends to raucous poker parties in the White House, at which large sums of money were gambled. He also drank rather heavily, something that Coolidge scorned.

Worst of all Harding's personal faults, though, was the fact that he was known to be having a love affair with a woman named Nan Britton, even though he was married. He and Nan even had a child. For these reasons, although the Coolidges had visited the Hardings at their home in Ohio after the Republican convention, the President and his Vice-President spent little time together apart from their official duties.

Harding and Coolidge probably saw each other most regularly at Cabinet meetings. Harding had invited Coolidge to attend these sessions, at which the President discussed issues with the heads (secretaries) of the major administrative departments of the government. Coolidge did not contribute much to the Cabinet meetings. He probably kept his eyes and ears open and learned how the government was being run, but, in typical "Silent Cal" fashion, he kept his opinions to himself.

THE TEAPOT DOME SCANDAL

Today, historians generally agree that Harding was not a very good President. He was poorly suited for the job because he knew very little about some important subjects, such as the national economy, and he did not care to apply the concentration and effort that would have been required to master them. He seems not to have liked being President very much. Once he told Nan Britton that being in the White House was like being in prison. "I'm in jail, and I can't get out!" he exclaimed, and he described himself as "a man of limited talents from a small town," who was not comfortable on the large stage of national and world events.

But Harding's gravest flaw as President was that, although he was personally honest about money, he foolishly allowed himself to be taken advantage of by friends and associates who were criminally dishonest. The result was a scandal that tainted Harding's presidency—and probably contributed to his death. This scandal, called the Teapot Dome Affair, developed slowly and secretly during the first 2½ years of the Harding-Coolidge administration.

Teapot Dome was the name given to one of three large underground oil deposits that were owned by the government. They were called the Naval Oil Reserves because they were initially intended to provide a back-up source of fuel for Navy vessels. Teapot Dome was a 90,000-acre tract of land in Wyoming; the other two reserves, Elk Hills and Buena Vista Hills, were both located in California.

Leasing Oil Reserves

In 1920, while Woodrow Wilson was still President, Congress decided that the government could make some money by leasing oil rights on the reserves—that is, by allowing private oil companies to drill on them in return for payments to the government. Congress ruled that the Navy Department would handle the leasing business.

The trouble started in November of that year, just two weeks after Harding and Coolidge were elected. Edward L. Doheny, a wealthy oil baron (as the millionaires who made their fortunes from drilling oil were then called), started negotiating with the U.S. government to develop some wells on the Teapot Dome reserve.

A Dishonest Insider

In order for the oil barons to get the leases they wanted on favorable terms, it was vitally important for them to have someone working on their behalf inside the Harding administration. They found a willing tool in Albert Fall of New Mexico, who was selected by Harding to serve in his Cabinet as secretary of the Interior Department. Fall then persuaded Edwin Denby, the secretary of the Navy Department, to ask President Harding to transfer the administration of the oil leases from the Navy to the Interior Department. Harding did so, apparently without question.

Within two months after the transfer, a lease was signed for the Elk Hills reserve. Four months later, Doheny "loaned" Albert Fall $10,000, which was delivered to Fall's home in a small satchel that was later called "the little black bag." And less than a month after that, Harry F. Sinclair of the Sinclair Oil Company, one of Doheny's associates, visited Fall's home in New Mexico and there began negotiating for the Teapot Dome reserve.

The exploitation of publicly owned oil did not go unnoticed. In March of 1922, the director of the Federal Bureau of Mines pointed out the loss of government oil income through private drilling, and a Navy captain wrote to Denby protesting against private profit-making at the cost of Navy oil. Senator Robert La Follette of Wisconsin asked the Senate to form a committee to investigate the whole question of oil leases.

Less than a week later, the Teapot Dome lease was signed by secretaries Denby and Fall, although it was kept a secret at the time. Fall even denied in public that the lease existed. But over the next few months, Sinclair gave $133,000 worth of bonds to Fall's son-in-law. These bonds, which had the same value as cash, eventually made their way into Fall's possession.

Bribery and Corruption

By the summer of 1922, the newspapers and congressional inquiries had stirred up considerable public interest in the oil leases. Hoping to calm the situation down, President Harding told the American people that he had personally approved all the leases. But Harding did not know about Fall's private arrangements with Doheny and Sinclair. In December of 1922, Fall and Doheny signed a second lease for Elk Hills. A few weeks later, Sinclair gave Fall's son-in-law a $25,000 cash "loan" in a Washington hotel room.

At about that same time, Fall realized that the Senate inquiries would soon reveal his part in the manipulation of the oil leases. He also knew that he would be unable to secure any more leases for his powerful friends, because the pressure of public scrutiny had grown too great. So he resigned from his post as secretary of the interior to take up what he called "private business interests." Soon after, Harry Sinclair "loaned" Fall another $50,000.

This seedy plot to abuse the country's oil reserves and to betray the public trust did not become known all at once. But by the summer of 1923, after Fall's resignation, Washington was buzzing with talk of bribery, corruption, and even possible criminal prosecution of the guilty parties.

Free of Scandal

No hint of scandal, however, attached itself to Vice-President Coolidge, who was not involved in the Teapot Dome affair in any way. This is not surprising, in view of his strict honesty. Some historians have found it surprising, though, that he never discussed the oil leases, even when the scandal was spread over the front pages of America's newspapers, and that he did not mention them once in his autobiography.

But Coolidge's honesty was the kind that concerned itself solely with his own doings and ignored what other people were up to. In addition, Coolidge was too shrewd a politician to make enemies within his party or his administration by getting involved in trouble when he could easily stay out of it. So he said nothing and did nothing as the Teapot Dome scandal simmered and hissed and got ready to boil over.

VERMONT SUMMER

The leaders of the government traditionally leave Washington, D.C., during the late summer, and 1923 was no exception. Harding went west on a speaking tour that was to take him through many western states; he also planned a vacation in Alaska. The Coolidges, too, were on vacation. Their older son, John, was a trainee at a military camp in Massachusetts, and Calvin, Jr., was working as a tobacco picker during his summer break from classes at Mercersburg Academy in Penn-

Wearing his grandfather's old smock, Coolidge placidly worked on the family farm in Plymouth while the beleaguered President Harding toured the western states. (Library of Congress.)

sylvania. Coolidge and Grace went north to visit old Colonel Coolidge and to catch the mountain breezes in Plymouth Notch.

It was a peaceful and relaxed summer for Coolidge. Wearing an old gray smock (a long, loose shirt) of the kind that had been worn by Vermont farmers since the Revolution, he puttered in the fields and around the farm buildings. Grace cooked the family meals in the simple kitchen. Photographers from newspapers and magazines frequently stopped by Plymouth Notch to snap a picture of the Vice-President in these countrified surroundings, and he posed agreeably for them. Some newsmen were even invited to sit down to dinner with the Coolidges. The meal was always plain food: meat and potatoes and maybe some fresh vegetables from the garden.

Coolidge had an opportunity to see friends and neighbors from his childhood. As always, though, he made no great show of his emotions. One day he was sitting on his front porch with a newsman when a man rode by in a wagon.

"Howdy, Cal!" the man called out.

"Howdy, Newt!" the Vice-President replied. Then, as the wagon passed on down the road, Coolidge turned to the fellow sitting next to him and calmly explained, "Cousin of mine. Haven't seen him for twenty years."

A Troubled President

While Coolidge was enjoying the pleasures of country life, Harding was having a less enjoyable time of it in the western states. He was scheduled to make a speech in Kansas City, but before the speech he was approached by the wife of Albert Fall, who talked privately with him for half an hour or so. Afterward, his aides noticed that the President seemed troubled and distracted. The next day Harding remarked that he did not have much trouble from his enemies — it was his friends who were the problem.

By this time Harding knew that Fall's misdeeds would soon be exposed, for La Follette and his investigating committee were on Fall's trail. Harding had also learned that the oil companies had secretly (and illegally) made large sums of money available to the national committee of the Republican Party, and this too, he feared, was soon to become public knowledge. He also feared that, although he was personally innocent of any direct wrongdoing, his reputation would be ruined beyond repair by these scandals. Perhaps he was even afraid he would be impeached (thrown out of office).

Perplexed and worried, Harding moved on to Alaska. There a private airplane brought him a long message in code. After reading it, the President nearly collapsed. He returned to Seattle, Washington, where he became ill. His aides announced that he had been stricken with food poisoning, but a later investigation showed this to be unlikely. He was moved to the Palace Hotel in San Francisco. There he was attended by doctors, who announced that the President had developed penumonia.

SUCCEEDING TO THE PRESIDENCY

In Plymouth Notch, the Coolidges had retired early to bed on the night of August 2. They planned to leave the farm the next day for a visit to Coolidge's friend, Frank Stearns, and his wife in Massachusetts. Their plans were changed suddenly late that night.

It was after midnight when a car pulled up to the Coolidge house and three men — Coolidge's secretary, his chauffeur, and a reporter — leaped out and pounded on the door. When Colonel Coolidge answered, they breathlessly told him that the President was dead. They had received the news by telegraph at Bridgewater, some miles away, and they had come by car to notify the Vice-President because the farm had no telephone.

The old colonel woke his son and daughter-in-law, who read two messages by lamplight. One was from Harding's secretary, telling Coolidge that the President had died at about 7:30 that evening (the cause of his death was never established for certain, but it seems to have been an embolism — a blood clot in an artery). A second message, from Harry Daugherty, the U.S. attorney general, urged Coolidge to hasten the necessary arrangements to be sworn in as President.

An Unusual Inauguration

By 2:30 in the morning of August 3, Plymouth Notch was aswarm with reporters who had driven there from nearby towns and with curious neighbors. Everyone expected that

By the flickering light of a kerosene lamp in the sitting room of the Plymouth home, Coolidge (on the left, with hand raised) was sworn in as President by his father following President Harding's death. (The Calvin Coolidge Memorial Foundation.)

Coolidge would set off at once for Washington, where he would be sworn into office by a member of the U.S. Supreme Court. But Coolidge saw no reason to rush about. After all, his own father was a justice of the peace and a notary public.

So, at 2:47 in the morning of August 3, 1923, in a small sitting room in his father's farmhouse, Calvin Coolidge was sworn in as 30th President of the United States by his father. A local congressman, a railway executive, an Army captain from Springfield, an official of the Springfield American Legion post, a newspaper editor, and a few members of Coolidge's staff were the witnesses.

The brief and subdued ceremony was as different from the usual pageantry and carnival of a presidential inauguration as anything could be. (Several weeks later, he was sworn in again in his hotel room in Washington by a member of the Supreme Court.) Grace Coolidge cried softly throughout. When the formal phrases had been spoken, Coolidge placed his hand on the Bible and said, "So help me God." Then he hugged his wife, shook his father's hand, and went to the dining room, where he dictated to his secretary a short statement to the nation.

Coolidge promised to do his best to fulfill the demands of the nation's highest office, and he asked the members of Harding's Cabinet to remain in their positions to help him. He ended by saying that "God will direct the destinies of our nation." Then, in his typical, matter-of-fact way, he blew out the lamp and went back to sleep.

Chapter 8

"Keep Cool with Coolidge"

O n the first day of his presidency, Coolidge rose early and crossed the road to the small family burial ground on the farm that had belonged to his grandfather, Galusha Coolidge. There he stood for a few silent moments in front of his mother's tombstone. Then he returned to the farm, and he and Grace set off by car for Rutland, where they could take a train to New York City and then on to Washington.

The Coolidges went by train from Washington to Marion, Ohio, where Harding was to be buried. The dead President was greatly mourned by the American people, who seem to have realized that he was a likable man, although a weak one. In the tragedy of Harding's sudden death, the Coolidges did not attract a great deal of public attention.

CLOSE FRIENDS

During the train ride to Marion, however, Coolidge was pestered by dozens of congressmen who had favors to ask — such as that a friend be appointed to fill a certain vacant position. Coolidge was glad that he and Grace had brought along their old friends, Frank Stearns and his wife, for more pleasant company. The Stearnses were to remain close to the Coolidges throughout their time in the White House.

Also present on the funeral train was William Howard Taft, a former Republican President who was now the Chief Justice of the Supreme Court. From the start of Coolidge's presidency, Taft offered good advice when it was requested without expecting favors in return. Coolidge generally respected Taft's judgment and enjoyed his company, and the two men were to become good friends.

After the funeral, the Coolidges returned to Washington—but not to the White House. They insisted that Mrs. Harding must be given all the time she wanted to pack her belongings and move out of the President's residence, so they moved back into their rooms at the New Willard Hotel. Ten days later, Mrs. Harding moved out and the Coolidges moved in. After they had walked into the grand hallway of the White House and gazed about them, Coolidge said to Grace, as calmly as if they were at home in Plymouth Notch or Northampton, "Now you run along upstairs."

Coolidge then spoke for a moment to Irwin H. Hoover, the head of the White House staff, who had served many Presidents. His only new instruction was this: "I don't want the public in our family rooms on the second floor so much as they have been." Privacy and simplicity would continue to be the chief characteristics of Coolidge's life while he lived in the White House, just as they had been for the previous 51 years.

THE FIRST YEAR

Coolidge soon settled into a routine and a way of life that he followed throughout his time in the White House. He had been a heavy sleeper all his life, and as President he usually slept for about 11 hours each day—nine hours or so at night and a two-hour nap in the middle of each afternoon. When newspapermen ridiculed or criticized his naps, he remarked that the naps were good for the country because he couldn't start any trouble while he was asleep. He used to wake up from them and ask his aide, "Is the country still here?"

Irwin Hoover wrote in his book, *Forty-Two Years in the White House,* that Coolidge worked shorter hours and did less work than any President he had observed. And H. L. Mencken, a newspaperman with a sharp tongue and a dislike for the President, once exclaimed, "Coolidge! A remarkable man. Nero fiddled while Rome burned, but Coolidge only snores."

Coolidge liked to go to bed early and get up early. Most days he rose at about 6:30 in the morning and strolled about the White House lawns and gardens before the servants and the rest of the household awoke. One night when he went to see the Marx Brothers in their play *Animal Crackers,* Groucho Marx spotted him in the audience and called out from the stage, "Isn't it past your bedtime, Calvin?"

War Whoops in the White House

The Coolidges regularly attended Sunday services at the First Congregational Church in Washington. As far as recreation was concerned, the President took walks, usually several a day, and he liked to fish. He and Grace used the presidential yacht, the *Mayflower,* for weekend excursions. They also vacationed in Massachusetts, New York State, Wisconsin, Georgia, and the Black Hills of South Dakota.

Coolidge had always enjoyed horseback riding, and as President he had a mechanical horse installed in the White House. Visitors recalled that he usually sat on it in solemn quiet while it joggled him up and down, but that occasionally he would utter piercing war whoops and wave his hat in his hand like a cowboy.

Coolidge's health was fairly good, although he suffered from asthma, hay fever, and frequent stomach aches. As time went on, he became dependent upon nasal sprays for his swollen sinuses, and he experimented with a number of pills and potions intended to relieve his upset digestive system.

There were no children in the White House during the Coolidge administration. John and Calvin, Jr., both lived away from home at Mercersburg Academy, a private high school. John graduated from Mercersburg in 1924 and then went on to Amherst College, his father's former school.

The Coolidges did, however, have company in the White House. They invited their old friends, Frank Stearns and his wife, to live with them, and the Stearnses often ate dinner with the President and the First Lady. Frank Stearns was always on hand if Coolidge felt like company in his study in the evenings. These companionable sessions were often rather silent, as Stearns and the President did not talk much. But it made Coolidge happy to relax and smoke a cigar with a friend who was not a member of the government.

Pets in the White House

Two features of the Coolidge administration were especially notable to members of the White House staff: pets and practical jokes. Coolidge loved animals. He and Grace kept a varying number of dogs, cats, birds, and even a pet racoon in the family portion of the White House. Coolidge's favorite pet was a large yellow cat that used to drape itself around his shoulders like a fur and ride from room to room. An admirer of the President once sent him a captive bear. Coolidge reluctantly agreed that he could not possibly keep it at the White

House, so he gave it to the Washington Zoo and visited it often to make sure that the zookeepers were taking good care of it.

His pets provided some amusement for Coolidge, and so did his practical jokes. They were rather silly jokes, but he found them funny. One of his favorites was to press buttons in his office that sounded buzzers all over the White House. Servants and aides would hasten to him from wherever they were working, only to find that he would pretend he had not rung for them, or that he had stepped out for a walk.

Thrift and Honesty

One other aspect of White House life that was noteworthy during the Coolidge years was the famous Coolidge way with money. The President was as thrifty as always. He hated waste, even though it would now be paid for by the taxpayers rather than out of his own pocket.

The White House cook recalled that Coolidge would come poking around the kitchen to be sure that food was not being wasted or used extravagantly. On one occasion, when guests were expected for a formal state dinner, the President wandered into the kitchen and noticed that the cook was preparing *six* hams. He was outraged. The cook reminded him that 60 people would be coming for dinner. He wandered off, shaking his head doubtfully, and said, "Six hams still seems like a lot to me." This particular cook resigned shortly thereafter.

In addition to his thriftiness (or stinginess, as some people called it), Coolidge retained his fundamental, careful honesty where money was concerned. He turned over to the government all the gifts that he received in office, and he and Grace paid for their vacations out of their private funds.

THE PRESIDENT'S CABINET

One task faced by all new Presidents is that of organizing their Cabinet. Coolidge hoped that the Cabinet members who had been appointed by Harding would continue in their posts, but eventually he had to make his own appointments to many departments as Cabinet members resigned or were transferred to other positions.

The Cabinet was very important in Coolidge's administration because he left more decisions and activities up to his Cabinet members than most other Presidents had done. Instead of directing them, he relied upon them for information and direction. Fortunately, his Cabinet did include some gifted and energetic members.

One Cabinet member who remained from Harding's administration all the way through Coolidge's was Andrew Mellon of Pennsylvania, the secretary of the treasury. He shared Coolidge's firm belief that "the business of America is business," and he favored laws that made it easy for large companies to expand and profit. Mellon also played a large part in designing several new tax laws that greatly lowered the taxes of the wealthy.

Harry S. New of Indiana, another holdover from Harding's Cabinet, was Coolidge's postmaster general. His principal contribution was to extend airmail service to more parts of the nation. James J. Davis of Pennsylvania, also a Harding administration holdover, was Coolidge's secretary of labor. He was not active in the administration.

Coolidge's secretary of commerce for most of his presidency was Herbert Hoover of California, who had been appointed by Harding. When Hoover resigned in 1928 to run for President, William Whiting of Massachusetts was appointed secretary of commerce for the final year of Coolidge's administration.

Harding's secretary of agriculture, Henry C. Wallace of Iowa, stayed on under Coolidge. He died in 1924 and was replaced by Howard M. Gore, who resigned after four months to become governor of West Virginia. Coolidge's third and final secretary in this Cabinet post was William Jardine of Kansas, who was the president of the Agricultural College of Manhattan, Kansas.

John Weeks of Massachusetts, secretary of war, served until 1925, when he was replaced by his assistant, Dwight F. Davis of Missouri. Davis, who had been an eager tennis player in his youth, is remembered today as the founder of the Davis Cup Trophy, one of the most prized championships in international tennis.

Edwin Denby, Harding's secretary of the navy, resigned in 1924 during the Senate investigation of the Teapot Dome scandal. Most historians believe that Denby was not guilty of direct participation in the money-making scheme but that he acted foolishly in allowing Albert Fall to take over the leases for the Naval Oil Reserves. Denby was replaced by Curtis D. Wilbur of California, whose greatest contribution was to encourage the Navy to add more aircraft to its fleet.

Albert Fall himself, Harding's ill-fated secretary of the interior, had been replaced by Hubert Work of Colorado before Coolidge became President. Work remained in the Cabinet until 1928, when he resigned to work in Hoover's presidential campaign. Roy O. West of Illinois replaced him.

Harding's choice for secretary of state, Charles Evans Hughes of New York, served in that post until 1925, when he resigned to resume his private law practice. Coolidge replaced Hughes with Frank B. Kellogg of Minnesota.

Harding had filled the final Cabinet position, that of attorney general (head of the Justice Department), with one of his old friends from Ohio, Harry M. Daugherty. Coolidge replaced Daugherty with Harlan Stone in 1924. Stone reorganized the Justice Department's Federal Bureau of Investigation (the FBI) and made a 29-year-old lawyer named J. Edgar Hoover the director of the FBI. Hoover was to play an increasingly large role in American politics and law enforcement over the following four decades. In 1925 Stone resigned from the Cabinet to accept Coolidge's appointment to the Supreme Court. His replacement as attorney general was John G. Sargent of Vermont.

The End of a Scandal

One of the biggest problems that Coolidge had to deal with upon becoming President was the Teapot Dome affair. His goal was to get the situation under control with as little lasting damage to the public image of the Republican Party as possible. To do this, he stayed out of the matter as much as he could, never referring to it or discussing it in his speeches.

Coolidge let a congressional committee handle the investigation into the Teapot Dome affair. This committee recommended that some of the people who had been involved in the scandal should be prosecuted under the law. Eventually, both Albert Fall and Harry Sinclair of Sinclair Oil went to jail; Edward Doheny, however, did not, as no crime could be proved against him. The illegal oil leases were cancelled, and the uproar in the nation's newspapers began to die down.

The only point at which Coolidge was forced to take direct action in cleaning up the Teapot Dome mess occurred in connection with Harry Daugherty, his first attorney general. Many people in the Senate and elsewhere felt that Daugherty, as an old friend of Harding's, had wanted to spare Harding any embarrassment. This was why Daugherty had not allowed the Justice Department to become involved in the investigation of the scandal.

Although it was not generally believed that Daugherty had been personally involved in Teapot Dome, it was widely felt that he had known about it and had done nothing to stop it. There were calls for his resignation, but he refused to resign. A number of Coolidge's supporters advised him to fire Daugherty, but he was reluctant to do this without firm proof of any wrongdoing. He did, however, hope that Daugherty would resign and gave him many hints about this, but Daugherty ignored them.

Finally, Coolidge realized that by keeping Daugherty in his Cabinet he was in danger of smearing his administration and his party with the scandal, which showed no sign of dying down as long as Daugherty remained in office. But Coolidge needed a definite reason to dismiss Daugherty. He found one when the attorney general refused to turn some of his department's papers over to the congressional investigating committee. Coolidge thereupon dismissed Daugherty from the Cabinet, and from that time on the public's confidence in the presidency was restored.

To the American people, Coolidge was the perfect example of personal honesty, upright moral values, and clean living—just what the country needed in the White House after the Harding administration.

THE ELECTION OF 1924

After Harding's death, Coolidge served as President for little more than a year before the presidential election of 1924. Like most men who have risen to the presidency through the death of a President, he was eager to be elected in his own right. He therefore made it clear from his early days in office that he planned to be his party's candidate for President the following year.

Coolidge was not universally popular among the Republicans. One group of party leaders felt that he had become overly influenced by big business and that he was not active enough. But he was popular with the general public, because his air of calmness and quiet seemed soothing after the horrors of the Great War and the uneasy excitement of the Harding years. Those Republicans who might have hoped to nominate someone else soon realized that no other candidate could win enough votes to be elected. So, when Republicans from around the country gathered at their national convention in Cleveland in June of 1924, no one was surprised when Coolidge was nominated for President.

The vice-presidential candidate chosen by the delegates was Charles C. Dawes of Illinois, a colorful person who had been a lawyer, a banker, and a brigadier general in World War I. In 1924 Dawes served as chairman of a congressional committee that examined the ruined economies of Germany and other European nations that had been devastated by the war. His recommendations regarding loans and aid to Europe, with the goal of helping the European countries (including Germany) re-establish stable and productive economies, came to be called the Dawes Plan. He won the Nobel Peace Prize for it.

In November voters went to the polls to choose between Republicans Coolidge and Dawes and Democrats John W. Davis of West Virginia and Charles W. Bryan of Nebraska. Robert La Follette of Wisconsin also ran for President as the candidate of a small, short-lived third party called the Progressives. The Republican campaign had used the slogan "Keep Cool with Coolidge" and had stressed Coolidge's favorite saying: "The business of America is business." Coolidge won by a landslide victory. He received 15,725,016 popular votes to 8,386,503 for the Democrats and 4,822,856 for the Progressives.

Charles Dawes, Coolidge's Vice-President, had already had several careers before entering politics. He won a Nobel Peace Prize for his plan to rebuild the war-torn economies of European nations. (Library of Congress.)

A Bitter Victory

Tragically, the election victory for which Coolidge had hoped brought him little happiness. His younger son, Calvin, Jr., died during the campaign. While playing tennis in tennis shoes without socks, he had developed a blister, which in turn led to blood poisoning. The boy became ill and no treatment could save him.

Calvin lay on his deathbed for four days, fighting a high fever and delirium, while the President held his hand or tried to bring a smile to his son's face with a baby rabbit from the garden. In the end, however, Calvin died. He was 14 years old. His death was a great blow to Coolidge, who later wrote, "When he went, the power and the glory of the presidency went with him."

In November of 1924, once the election was over and the Coolidges knew that they would be living in the White House for another four years, Grace Coolidge devoted herself to easing the grief-stricken President's burden. She is still remembered as one of the most charming and gracious hostesses the White House has ever had. She made extra efforts to see that everything was done the way Coolidge liked it and that visitors had pleasant experiences. In the privacy of her sitting room, however, she began to crochet a new bedspread, which would be made up of 48 squares of needlework—one for each month that the Coolidges had to remain in Washington before they could return to Northampton and private life.

Chapter 9

Roaring Twenties President

Coolidge's presidency took place during one of the liveliest decades in U.S. history—the 1920s, sometimes called the Roaring Twenties. It was a time of feverish activity and also of many changes in American life.

One reason for the fast pace of life in the Roaring Twenties was the end of the Great War and the return of U.S. soldiers from overseas. It is as though the American people wanted to put the suffering and grim events of the war out of mind with an emphasis on money and pleasure.

There was a burst of activity in the field of popular entertainment. The film industry, which began in the United States around 1908, grew rapidly to satisfy the public's demand for movies. Stars like Greta Garbo, Charlie Chaplin, and Rudolph Valentino created Hollywood legends, and movies took a giant step forward in 1927, during Coolidge's administration, when the first "talkie," or motion picture with sound, was produced.

Radios became common in American homes (the 1924 Republican National Convention was the first to be broadcast on the radio), and new forms of popular music such as jazz appeared. So did fashionable dances such as the fast-moving Charleston. Women wore their hair and their dresses shorter than ever before, and men bought new cars by the thousands.

THE PROHIBITION ERA

All of this excitement happened while the United States was experimenting with a new social policy. Ever since the mid-1800s, certain portions of the public had been opposed to the sale and use of alcoholic drinks. This antialcohol movement gained strength in the early years of the 20th century, and many states passed laws that made it illegal to sell, buy, or drink alcohol. Finally, the Constitution was amended to make alcohol illegal across the entire country, beginning in 1920. The law that changed the Constitution was called the Prohibition Act, because it prohibited (banned) alcohol. This is why the Roaring Twenties are also sometimes called the Prohibition Era.

Prohibition was not a success. Instead of giving up alcoholic drinks, hundreds of thousands of law-abiding Americans who could no longer legally purchase liquor took to breaking the law. They bought liquor from smugglers, called rum-runners, who used speedboats to bring supplies in from ships at sea. The smugglers often worked for organized crime gangs such as that of Al Capone in Chicago. In this way, Prohibition brought about an increase in crime and criminal organizations, because the nation's police forces were simply not large enough to enforce this new and unpopular law. President Coolidge supported Prohibition and strictly observed it, but the law-enforcement problems of Prohibition caused continual trouble for his attorney generals.

A federal agent destroys a shipment of liquor during Prohibition, when it was illegal to manufacture, distribute, or sell alcoholic beverages in the United States. (Library of Congress.)

MOSTLY ABOUT MONEY

Economic problems were building throughout the country during Coolidge's presidency. On the surface, the United States seemed more prosperous than ever. Factories were producing goods, railroads were spreading, and huge sums of money were changing hands on the stock market. But beneath the surface, the financial state of the country was not so healthy. Banks were making millions of dollars' worth of loans, mostly to foreign countries, that were never paid back. As the 1920s went on, hundreds of large and small banks began to fail, or close, and many ordinary people lost their savings.

And while there was little unemployment, wages were so high that many companies could not afford to pay their workers. This was because the country's industries had raised wages during the war in order to attract workers into companies that produced metals, weapons, and other war goods. Now that the war was over, no one wanted to take a cut in pay, so employers had to pay high wages. This meant that they had to charge more for the goods they produced, which meant, in turn, that the cost of living started to rise.

A Faltering Economy

At the same time, the American farm industry began to suffer. The government had paid steady prices for agricultural products during the war. Once that practice was stopped, many farmers found their earnings falling. In addition, in 1924 the Coolidge government passed an immigration act that greatly reduced the number of people who were allowed to come into the United States from other countries to live and work. In 1927 the immigration quota was lowered again, to only 150,000 people each year (663,000 people had entered the country in 1924, before the immigration act was passed). This lowering of immigration meant a loss of labor for the nation's railroads and factories. To fill the need, many farmers left their

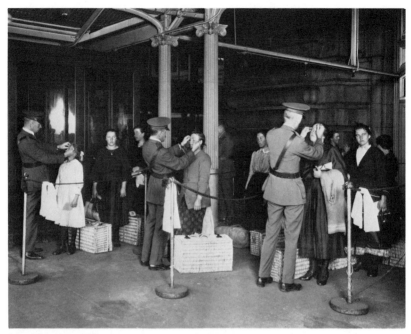

Most foreigners who came to start a new life in America entered the United States at Ellis Island in New York, where they were inspected for disease before being allowed to proceed. Coolidge's administration drastically lowered the number of immigrants permitted to enter the country each year. (National Archives.)

homesteads and moved to the cities, feeling that farm life offered no future. Food production became unstable.

Many economic advisors felt that the government should become more involved in planning and controlling the economy. But it was Coolidge's firm belief that business was business and government was government, and that the two should not be mixed. He felt that everyone had the best chance to prosper when the government was least involved in the economy, and he thought that economic problems, including the farm problem, would sort themselves out in time if they were left alone.

Coolidge voted against congressional bills to provide aid to farmers and against a bill to give a cash bonus to returning soldiers. In fact, Coolidge is remembered today as the President who sat in the White House and did almost nothing to head off the economic disaster that would overtake the country almost as soon as he left office.

Milestones of the Coolidge Years

Although Coolidge was something of a "do-nothing" President, his years in office saw many milestones in American history. One occurred in 1925, just five years after the first election in which women voted for a President, when Nellie Tayloe Ross of Wyoming became the first woman governor in the United States.

Some milestones involved the new science of flying. In July of 1924, the first regular airmail service to span the whole country, from New York to Los Angeles, was started. In 1926 the Coolidge administration passed the Air Commerce Act, which gave the federal government the right to oversee air traffic (it does so today through the Federal Aviation Administration, or FAA). And in 1927 a young man named Charles Lindbergh became the hero of America and the world when he made the first solo flight across the Atlantic Ocean, from New York to Paris. The biggest social event of Washington during Coolidge's time was a party that the Coolidges gave at the White House to honor Lindbergh.

Another glittering occasion in the nation's capital was a state banquet for Queen Marie of Romania. She was the first reigning queen ever entertained at the White House, and diamond jewelry and elaborate gowns were everywhere, perhaps somewhat dazzling the homespun Coolidges. But the nation's biggest social event was probably the Sesquicentennial Exhibition, a huge fair held in Philadelphia, Pennsylvania, in 1926 to celebrate the 150th birthday of the United States. It was an occasion for the country to take pride in the best of its arts, sciences, industries, and entertainments.

Lucky Lindy

Charles Lindbergh was probably the best-known pilot who ever flew a plane—and certainly the best loved. He learned to fly in Texas in 1924 and became one of the country's first airmail pilots in 1926. A prize of $25,000 had been offered to the first pilot who could complete a nonstop flight from New York to Paris, and in 1927 Lindbergh obtained a plane called "The Spirit of St. Louis" and made the flight. On May 20 and 21 in 33½ hours, Lindbergh became the first person to cross an ocean by air; he also became a hero on two continents. The triumphant and admiring nickname of "Lucky Lindy" was in every newspaper and on everyone's lips.

When Lindbergh later flew nonstop from Washington to Mexico City, he met and fell in love with Anne Morrow, the daughter of U.S. Ambassador Dwight Morrow. The two were married, but tragedy touched their lives in 1932, when their two-year-old son was kidnapped and murdered. The Lindbergh case was the most talked-about crime of the 1930s, and the Lindberghs fled to Europe to escape the flood of painful publicity.

Lindbergh urged the United States to remain out of World War II, but when America entered the war, he served as an aircraft consultant and pilot in the Pacific. After the war, he and his family settled in Connecticut.

Through his work with the U.S. Department of Defense and the National Advisory Committee for Aeronautics, Lindbergh did

Shown here with the plane in which he made his epic solo flight across the Atlantic, Charles Lindbergh became a hero to Americans and Europeans alike. (National Archives.)

more than any other man to promote aviation science in the military and in industry. And through his thrilling adventures, he did more than any other pilot to turn the eyes and thoughts of Americans skyward. His book about the transatlantic crossing, *The Spirit of St. Louis*, was published in 1953. It won a Pulitzer Prize (a literary award) and became a best-seller.

FOREIGN AFFAIRS

President Wilson had wanted the United States to join the League of Nations, but most of the American people were opposed to the idea, and both Harding and Coolidge continued to keep the United States out of the League. Under Coolidge, the United States made its own independent terms with the new nations that were created when Germany and Austria-Hungary were broken up after the Great War. Among these nations were Poland, Yugoslavia, Latvia, Lithuania, Estonia, Finland, Czechoslovakia, Hungary, and Romania.

Protecting "U.S. Lives and Property"

Most of the international activity of Coolidge's administration took place in Latin America. The United States had become involved in the affairs of Nicaragua, in Central America, in 1912, when U.S. Marines were sent there to support a president who was favored by American business interests (mostly sugar and banana companies and some railroads). Although many Americans, including many members of Congress, felt that the United States had no right to interfere in the internal politics of a neighboring country, Coolidge continued the practice of Presidents Wilson and Harding by keeping about 50,000 Marines there to "protect U.S. lives and property," as this action was usually described.

The Marines strengthened the rule of President Adolfo Diaz, an ally of the United States. But a sizable number of Nicaraguans were opposed both to Diaz and to the presence of U.S. soldiers in their country. These rebels fought against the Marines when they could, led by a man named Augusto Sandino. The Marines finally overcame Sandino in 1928, and an election was held under U.S. supervision. Since that time, the United States has remained interested and involved in affairs in Nicaragua – but seldom as openly as in Coolidge's day. (The rebel leader Sandino's name lives on today in the name of Nicaragua's Sandinista Party.)

Problems with Mexico

Another hot spot for Coolidge in Latin America was Mexico. The United States had two reasons to be upset with its neighbor south of the border. First, the Mexican government and people wanted to end foreign ownership of the country's mines, many of which belonged to American industrialists. American businessmen were afraid that Mexico would seize their mines without paying them what the mines were worth, and Coolidge was determined not to let this happen.

Second, Mexicans in the southern part of Mexico were supplying weapons to the Sandino rebels in Nicaragua, and Coolidge wanted to end that, too. But Mexican President Plutarco Calles did not seem willing to come to a compromise agreement with the United States.

It was then, in 1927, that Coolidge carried out one of his shrewdest moves. He made his old Amherst friend, Dwight Morrow, the U.S. ambassador to Mexico. Morrow was friendly, tactful, humorous, and intelligent. He made a good impression on Calles and on the Mexican government, and soon the two nations reached agreement on a number of issues. Morrow invited Charles Lindbergh to fly nonstop from Washington to Mexico City as a symbol of the friendship between the two governments, and this made a big hit with the Mexican people. Relations between the United States and its southern neighbor were at their best under Morrow's guidance. His handling of the Mexican problem was one of Coolidge's true triumphs.

The Pact of Peace

One of the final landmarks of the Coolidge administration was the doing of Frank Kellogg, Coolidge's secretary of state. On April 6, 1927, the 10th anniversary of the date on which the United States entered the Great War, France's foreign minister suggested that France and the United States should enter into a treaty that would ban war and agree to settle all international disputes peacefully. This minister, Aristide Briand, drew up the treaty with Kellogg, who suggested that other nations be invited to sign it.

In August of 1928 Kellogg went to Paris, where he and representatives of 14 other countries signed the Briand-Kellogg Pact, also called the Pact of Peace and the Pact of Paris. Under this agreement, the following countries agreed not to make war: France, the United States, Germany, Belgium, Great Britain, Ireland, Canada, Australia, New Zealand, India, South Africa, Italy, Japan, Poland, and Czechoslovakia. Eventually, 47 more nations joined the agreement. Kellogg received the Nobel Peace Prize in 1929 for his work on the pact. Sadly, the international agreement did not prevent World War II from starting a decade later.

President Coolidge signs the Pact of Peace that was supposed to end all wars. On the right sits Secretary of State Frank Kellogg, who helped write the pact; U.S. senators stand behind them. (Library of Congress.)

NO RE-ELECTION

In the summer of 1927, the Coolidges took a vacation out West. As they were passing through the Black Hills of South Dakota on their way to Yellowstone National Park, President Coolidge made a surprising and unexpected announcement. Many Republicans expected him to run for President again in 1928.

But on August 3, Coolidge abruptly called a news conference in Rapid City, South Dakota, and declared, "I do not choose to run for President in 1928."

Just those 10 words — it was typical of Coolidge to use as few words as possible. He offered no explanation, then or ever. Some historians have felt that Coolidge decided not to run again because he was concerned about his failing health and Grace's well-being. Others suggest that he was afraid he might not be elected. Still others say that he foresaw the bad times that were in store for the country in the coming years and did not want to be President during them.

But whatever his reason, Coolidge was as unshakably firm as in all of his decisions. He would leave the White House in March of 1929.

Chapter 10

After the White House

The Republicans chose Herbert Hoover, the secretary of commerce in Coolidge's Cabinet, as their presidential candidate in 1928. Coolidge gave Hoover his support and was pleased when Hoover defeated Alfred Smith, the Democratic candidate, in November. The Coolidges then drifted through their final months in the White House. Grace added the last few squares to the needlework bedspread, the one with a square for every month of her husband's presidency.

Coolidge himself took more naps than ever and visited with friends. While Jim Lucey, his old shoemaker friend from Northampton, was a guest at the White House for dinner one day, Grace and Coolidge pumped him for news of home. It was clear that they were looking forward to stepping out of the spotlight of national leadership and returning to the privacy of Northampton.

It was at this time that Coolidge made a remark that is often quoted as the best example of his unique sense of humor. He had become famous as a man of very few words, and one hostess at a dinner party said to him, "You must sit next to me, Mr. President. I have a bet with a friend that I will get more than two words out of you." Coolidge looked her in the eye and said, "You lose."

One cartoonist linked Coolidge's decision not to run for re-election to his well-known fondness for a quiet, peaceful life.
(Library of Congress.)

Also during this period, Coolidge was besieged by businessmen offering him directorships of banks, railroads, newspapers, and the like. Coolidge turned down all offers. "These people are trying to hire not Calvin Coolidge, but a former President of the United States," he explained. "I can't make that kind of use of the office. I can't do anything that might take away from the presidency any of its dignity." He did, however, accept an offer from the Cosmopolitan Book Corporation to publish his memoirs. (This autobiography was published in 1929.)

BACK HOME AT LAST

On March 4, 1929, Coolidge attended the inauguration of Herbert Hoover. He then packed away the picture of his mother that had sat on his desk throughout his presidency, boarded a train with Grace, and returned to his small Massachusetts home and his law office.

Back in Northampton, Grace eagerly resumed her activities with the church, the Red Cross, and the women's clubs. Coolidge spent a lot of time in his study, working on his autobiography and on articles he wrote for two popular magazines, *The Saturday Evening Post* and *Collier's*. In 1930 and 1931, he wrote a weekly newspaper column called "Thinking Things Over with Calvin Coolidge."

Also in 1931, Coolidge made a radio appearance, warning listeners against fraudulent insurance agents. A man named Lewis Tibbett, an insurance agent in St. Louis, actually sued Coolidge for this speech, claiming that it had cost him $100,000 worth of business. Although Tibbett's claim was ridiculous, Coolidge did not want the bother and embarrassment of a jury trial, so he paid the man $2,500 to drop the case and leave him alone.

The Stock Market Crash of 1929

Events in the country and the world took a turn for the worse about the time Coolidge left office. The economic troubles that had been brewing beneath the surface appearance of prosperity finally burst upon the land in October 1929, when the New York stock market, the financial center of the nation, experienced a devastating crash. Thousands of shares in companies were sold for a fraction of their value because people sensed that the national economy was out of control. Overnight, hundreds of wealthy investors found themselves penniless. Many banks failed. Factories closed, and joblessness began to rise.

It was the beginning of an era of poverty and pessimism called the Great Depression — but now it was Hoover's problem. In 1932, a well-known actor named Otis Skinner said to Coolidge, "I wish you were running for President again. It would be the end of this terrible depression." Quick as a flash, Coolidge dryly replied, "It would be the beginning of mine."

On January 5, 1933, Coolidge spent the day doing a little paperwork at his office in the morning and then working on a crossword puzzle at home. At around noon, he went upstairs for a nap. Grace Coolidge found him sprawled on the floor an hour later, dead of a heart attack.

Funeral services for the former President were held at Edwards Congregational Church in Northampton. He was buried in the Coolidge family plot in Plymouth. Young John Coolidge stood at the gravesite with his mother. So did Frank Stearns and a few other close friends. At Grace's request, the preacher recited these lines:

> Warm summer sun,
> Shine kindly here;
> Warm southern wind,
> Blow softly here;
> Green sod above,
> Lie light, lie light.
> Goodnight, dear heart,
> Goodnight, goodnight.

COOLIDGE REMEMBERED

In the annals of American history, Presidents such as Washington, Jefferson, and Lincoln are remembered as exceptional heroes. A few, such as Harding and Nixon, are remembered as scoundrels or incompetents. But the majority of Presidents fall somewhere in the middle, not distinguished by great events, great virtues, or great faults. Coolidge is one of these.

Many people, especially during the economic crisis of the 1930s, blamed Coolidge for the Great Depression. They felt that he ought to have done something to prevent it. They also felt that he was too lazy and too unconcerned about very real troubles.

One who had this opinion was H. L. Mencken, a journalist who believed that Coolidge had carried laziness to the point of being an art form. He wrote that there was no way of knowing just how Coolidge would have reacted if the Depression had hit America a few years earlier, but he added, "My own [guess] is that he would have responded to bad times precisely as he responded to good ones – that is, by pulling down the blinds, stretching his legs upon his desk, and snoozing away the lazy afternoon."

Walter Lippman, another journalist, said in 1926 that Coolidge's inactivity was more than simple laziness. "It is a grim, determined, alert inactivity which keeps Mr. Coolidge occupied constantly," Lippman wrote.

One of the cruelest and funniest quips about Coolidge's inactivity was made by Dorothy Parker, a prominent writer and wit. When she was told that Coolidge was dead, she asked, "How can they tell?" And Coolidge himself gave strength to the stories of his "do-nothing" attitude when he said, "Four-fifths of all our troubles in this life would disappear if we would only sit down and keep still." He was good at that.

Despite such criticisms, the good things about Coolidge's presidency must not be overlooked. If he did not make strong moves for the better, at least he did not make any great mistakes. The country stayed out of war during his administration. Business, science, and industry were given a free hand to grow and develop. But his personal virtues were Coolidge's greatest contribution to the office he held: thrift, honesty, steadfast moral values, and simplicity.

A Democratic opponent, Alfred Smith, made one of the best judgments of Coolidge when he said:

> Mr. Coolidge belongs rather in the class of Presidents who were distinguished for character more than for heroic achievement. His great task was to restore the dignity and prestige of the presidency when it had reached the lowest ebb in our history and to afford, in a time of extravagance and waste, a shining public example of the simple and homely virtues which came down to him from his New England ancestors.

Bibliography

Abels, Joseph. *In the Time of Silent Cal.* New York: Putnam, 1969. Complete with illustrations, this volume offers a look at American life and culture during the years 1919 to 1933.

Lathem, Edward Connery, editor. *Meet Calvin Coolidge: The Man Behind the Myth.* Brattleboro, Vermont: Stephen Greene Press, 1960. This biography gives special emphasis to Coolidge's New England background. It contains many humorous stories and anecdotes about Coolidge's family and personal life.

McCoy, Donald R. *Calvin Coolidge.* New York: Macmillan, 1967. This 472-page book is the most up-to-date and thorough account of Coolidge's life and presidency.

McKee, John Hiram, compiler. *Coolidge Wit and Wisdom: 125 Short Stories About "Cal."* New York: Frederick A. Stokes, 1933. In this 145-page volume, McKee collected humorous and intimate stories about Coolidge gathered from friends, colleagues, and newspaper articles. Although not recommended for accuracy or factual information, the book is entertaining and colorful.

Murray, Robert K. *The Politics of Normalcy: Governmental Theory and Practice in the Harding-Coolidge Era.* New York: W. W. Norton, 1973. In spite of its serious-sounding title, this volume is a fairly brief (162 pages) overview of some of the political issues that occupied Harding's and Coolidge's presidencies.

White, William Allen. *A Puritan in Babylon: The Story of Calvin Coolidge.* New York: Macmillan, 1938. White, a famous newspaperman, wrote two books about Coolidge. The first was a short biography that was published during Coolidge's presidency. This volume was the second. It is a thoughtful study of Coolidge's life and times, based on personal knowledge of the President. White's lively, tongue-in-cheek writing style will delight some readers but may be confusing to others.

Index

PRESIDENTS OF THE UNITED STATES

GEORGE WASHINGTON	L. Falkof	0-944483-19-4
JOHN ADAMS	R. Stefoff	0-944483-10-0
THOMAS JEFFERSON	R. Stefoff	0-944483-07-0
JAMES MADISON	B. Polikoff	0-944483-22-4
JAMES MONROE	R. Stefoff	0-944483-11-9
JOHN QUINCY ADAMS	M. Greenblatt	0-944483-21-6
ANDREW JACKSON	R. Stefoff	0-944483-08-9
MARTIN VAN BUREN	R. Ellis	0-944483-12-7
WILLIAM HENRY HARRISON	R. Stefoff	0-944483-54-2
JOHN TYLER	L. Falkof	0-944483-60-7
JAMES K. POLK	M. Greenblatt	0-944483-04-6
ZACHARY TAYLOR	D. Collins	0-944483-17-8
MILLARD FILLMORE	K. Law	0-944483-61-5
FRANKLIN PIERCE	F. Brown	0-944483-25-9
JAMES BUCHANAN	D. Collins	0-944483-62-3
ABRAHAM LINCOLN	R. Stefoff	0-944483-14-3
ANDREW JOHNSON	R. Stevens	0-944483-16-X
ULYSSES S. GRANT	L. Falkof	0-944483-02-X
RUTHERFORD B. HAYES	N. Robbins	0-944483-23-2
JAMES A. GARFIELD	F. Brown	0-944483-63-1
CHESTER A. ARTHUR	R. Stevens	0-944483-05-4
GROVER CLEVELAND	D. Collins	0-944483-01-1
BENJAMIN HARRISON	R. Stevens	0-944483-15-1
WILLIAM McKINLEY	D. Collins	0-944483-55-0
THEODORE ROOSEVELT	R. Stefoff	0-944483-09-7
WILLIAM H. TAFT	L. Falkof	0-944483-56-9
WOODROW WILSON	D. Collins	0-944483-18-6
WARREN G. HARDING	A. Canadeo	0-944483-64-X
CALVIN COOLIDGE	R. Stevens	0-944483-57-7

HERBERT C. HOOVER	B. Polikoff	0-944483-58-5
FRANKLIN D. ROOSEVELT	M. Greenblatt	0-944483-06-2
HARRY S. TRUMAN	D. Collins	0-944483-00-3
DWIGHT D. EISENHOWER	R. Ellis	0-944483-13-5
JOHN F. KENNEDY	L. Falkof	0-944483-03-8
LYNDON B. JOHNSON	L. Falkof	0-944483-20-8
RICHARD M. NIXON	R. Stefoff	0-944483-59-3
GERALD R. FORD	D. Collins	0-944483-65-8
JAMES E. CARTER	D. Richman	0-944483-24-0
RONALD W. REAGAN	N. Robbins	0-944483-66-6
GEORGE H.W. BUSH	R. Stefoff	0-944483-67-4

GARRETT EDUCATIONAL CORPORATION
130 EAST 13TH STREET
ADA, OK 74820